VISAS FOR FRANCE

BY

ISABELLA BIRD

Copyright © 2025 World's Eye

All rights reserved.

ISBN: 979-10-977147-0-3

Welcome to Your French Visa Journey	6
Ready, Steady, Go!	11
Non-Working Visas	16
Visas for Employment	23
Visas for Self-Employment/Setting Up a Business	33
Visas for Spouses, Partners and Family	43
Digital Nomads and Remote Working	50
Visas for running a Gite or Chambre D'Hotes	56
Qualifications	64
The Application Process	71
Here Comes the Paperwork!	79
Making Sure You Have	79
the Correct Documents	79
Trouble-Shooting TLS	85
Photograph Requirements	94
Health Insurance	99
How to Write a Covering Letter	104
How to Handle Delays and Rejections	110
Let's Go	118
The French Healthcare System for New Residents	124
Registering a Business in France	133
Language Test and Integration into French Society	140

Renewing Your Visa/Carte de Séjour   145

Key Terminology   151

for Visas   151

A Word from the Author   157

Welcome to Your French Visa Journey

I still get frustrated with admin after 23 years here , but wouldn't change a thing , space countryside , lovely people , food and wine

Whatever reasons you have for thinking about moving to France, the next few days, months or years will be exciting, challenging and sometimes downright scary.

However, take comfort in the fact that around 13,000 US citizens in 2024 managed to make their dream of moving to France a reality. So, it's certainly doable but first you will need to have the correct visa for your situation.

If the idea of visas makes you break into a cold sweat, don't worry - you're not alone.

French bureaucracy has a reputation for being overwhelming. There's usually lots of forms to complete, documents to provide, face-to-face appointments and lengthy waiting times to get things done. Newbies embarking on this journey can often feel as if they don't know where to start.

I've put together this user-friendly guide to help you navigate the tricky world of French visas in plain, simple English.

Why Have I written This Guide?

I've dedicated a huge amount of time to researching French visas, staying up to date with any changes, and helping others navigate the process. Consider me your visa-nerd friend who's here to make things as easy as possible for you.

I know there is already a lot of help out there, particularly on some social media groups set up for this specific purpose.

Although some of them have knowledgeable people who can give good advice, there are also a lot of groups where the advice and information given is poor or incomplete.

If you go to one of the groups to ask a question, you may be told to 'refer to the guides' they have provided. Those guides are often just extracts from official sources, which is good as the information is accurate, but not so good in that the guides are often written in difficult, legal language leaving you none the wiser.

This is why I have written this guide.

All the information in this guide comes from official or trusted sources and I have checked and rechecked all the facts (several times!) with extensive research and conversations with officials and other experts.

I have then tried to explain it all in plain English, hoping to make a complex subject a little less complicated.

As you read through the guide you'll see some real-life quotes from people who have made the journey to France before you.

I look forward to holding your hand on this exciting journey as you start to make your dreams for the next chapter of your life come true.

What to Expect from This Book

Keep it Simple is my motto for this book.

This book is written in plain English—no legal gobbledygook—so you can understand what you need to do without feeling like you need a law degree.

We'll break down everything you need to know, including:

- The different types of French visas (and which one is right for you!)
- The step-by-step application process
- What documents you need (and how to avoid common mistakes)
- The joys of French paperwork (okay, maybe not 'joys' but manageable).
- How to deal with delays, rejections, and other bumps in the road
- What happens once you arrive in France—because it doesn't stop when your visa is approved and you have the stamp in your passport.

Who Is This Book For?

Whether you're moving to France for a job, to study, to join family, or just to soak up the unique culture of France, this guide is for you.

Maybe you're new to the French visa system and have no idea where to begin? Don't worry, I've got you covered.
Are you already knee-deep in the visa process and feeling lost? I'll help you untangle the mess.

But with the right guidance (and a bit of patience), you can get through it.

A Quick Word on French Bureaucracy

Dealing with French administration can sometimes feel like trying to solve a puzzle where half the pieces are missing, and the instructions are in ancient Latin.

Just remember, a little organization, keeping your focus on your dream of moving to France and maybe a glass of wine can go a long way.

Ready to Get Started?

OK - let's take things step by step.

In the next chapter, we'll look at the different types of visas and help you figure out which one is the best fit for your situation.

Grab a notebook, make yourself a cup of coffee, tea, or pour a glass of wine and let's get your French adventure started!

Ready, Steady, Go!

Life is sweet, safe, my daughter and I get to enjoy the natural beauty of landscapes, the impromptu meetings in the old towns talking to people, getting a fresh croissant on our morning walk to school, taking the time to actually live and enjoy life.

Okay, let's be clear - France offers quite a few different types of visas, and choosing the right one is the first (and arguably the most important) step in your journey.

The visa you need depends on why you're moving to France and how long you plan to stay.

Things to consider include:

- Are you planning to work in France?
- Will you be retired and living off your pension?
- Is your plan to come as a student or to join a spouse already living in France?

Let's begin with a quick overview of the different types of visa.

At this point make a note of the ones that may apply to your specific situation so you know which ones to focus on. That way you will be able to see the wood for the trees.

1. Short-Stay Visa (Visa de Court Séjour)

This is also known as a Schengen Visa, and it's for stays of up to 90 days within a 180-day rolling period.

If you're planning a short-term trip for tourism, business, or visiting family and friends, this is the one for you. But, spoiler alert—it does not allow you to work in France or extend your stay beyond the 90 days.

US passport holders benefit from the Schengen Visa waiver meaning they can come to France (or any other country in the Schengen Zone) for a maximum of 90 days in a rolling 180 days without needing to apply for this or any other visa (unless they are coming to work).

It is not 90 days in each country but 90 days in the entire Schengen Zone.

At the time of writing this guide, there are plans to introduce a travel authorization which US passport holders will need to have when travelling to any of the 30 European countries specified.

The authorization will be known as ETIAS and the latest information is that it will be introduced in 2026.

ETIAS is not a visa, it is a travel authorization and does not guarantee entry into France or any of the other European countries.

You will still have to satisfy border control that you meet the other entry conditions for your visa or Schengen visa waiver stay (valid passport, minimum income etc).

2. Long-Stay Visa (Visa de Long Séjour)

If you're planning to stay in France for more than 90 days in a rolling 180 days, you'll need a long-stay visa.

This type of visa often doubles as a residence permit, but in some cases, you'll need to apply for an actual residence card once you arrive.

Here are the main categories of long-stay visas:

Work Visa

If you have a job offer in France, you'll likely need a work visa. There are different types depending on your profession and contract type:

- Salaried Employee Visa: For those with a French work contract.
- Talent Passport Visa: For highly skilled workers, entrepreneurs, and artists.
- Seasonal Worker Visa: For temporary or seasonal jobs (e.g., tourism or agriculture).

Student Visa

Studying in France? Lucky you! You'll need a Student Visa, which allows you to enrol in a French institution and even work part-time while studying.

Family Reunification Visa

If you're moving to join a spouse, parent, or child who is legally residing in France, you'll need a Family Visa.

The type depends on your situation, but in most cases, you'll need to prove your relationship and financial means.

Visitor Visa

This is for those who want to live in France without working. You'll need to prove that you have sufficient financial means to support yourself (pensions, savings, or passive income usually do the trick. (Note - you cannot use your 401K or IRA unless the money is immediately available).

Entrepreneur/Business Visa

Planning to start a business or work as a freelancer in France? The Entrepreneur Visa or Self-Employed Visa might be your best bet. Requirements vary, but you'll usually need to provide a solid business plan.

3. Permanent Residency & Citizenship

If you're in it for the long haul, you can apply for permanent residency after living in France for a certain number of years (usually five).

Citizenship? That's an even bigger commitment, but totally possible if you meet the requirements.

Next up: how to apply for your visa without losing your mind!

Non-Working Visas

> Only regret is we should have done it sooner.

There is a confusing selection of visa options and it is important you choose the correct one that best suits your circumstances.

As well as various visas that allow you to work, study, and set up a business, there are also visas for people who do not need or want to work and who have sufficient financial resources to support themselves and their family.

People who fit into this category are sometimes referred to as inactive (inactif) or FIPs (financially independent persons).

Don't be misled by the word *visiteur* that appears on these visas - even visas for those wishing to take up long-term residency and not work will have the word visiteur.

There are 2 visas for people who want to come to France for more than 3 months but do not want or need to work. They are the **VLS-T - Visiteur (visa de long séjour temporaire - visiteur)** and the **VLS-TS - Visiteur (visa de long séjour valant titre de séjour - visiteur)**.

The **VLS-T Visiteur** visa is for people who are certain that they will not extend their stay beyond the duration of their visa. This is non-renewable. You will have to return to the US on or before the expiry date.

The **VLS-TS Visiteur** visa is equivalent to a residence permit. It is usually valid for 4 - 12 months and can be renewed. It is usually for people who wish to take up residency.

For stays up to 90 Days - (Schengen Visa Waiver) - No Visa Required

Key Requirements

- You must hold a valid passport from a country that is exempt from requiring a visa for the Schengen Zone. The US is one of those countries. The passport must be a 10 year passport with 3 months validity left on the planned date of departure from France. The date of expiry is 10 years from the date of issue.
- You must have sufficient financial resources for the duration of your stay to travel and pay expenses and you must be able to prove it (personal bank statements for the last 3 months, last 3 pay slips, credit/debit cards statements, travelers cheques etc. You must prove financial resources for the duration of your stay as follows:

    - 65 euros per day if you can prove you have a hotel booking.
    - 120 euros per day if you do not have accommodation booked or cannot prove booked accommodation
    - If you only have a hotel booking for part of your stay you will need 65 euros per day for the days you have the booking and 120 euros for the days you have no booking).

Restrictions

- Stay is limited to 90 days in a rolling 180 days. There is a calculator to help you work out how many days you have spent in the Schengen Zone

and how many you have left. https://www.visa-calculator.com/
- If you are staying with a relative or friend you must have a certificate validated by the Mairie - Cerfa form no. 10798*03 - attestation d'accueil (your family member or friend must do this and send it to you). You must also show financial resources of €32.50 per day if asked by border control.
- You must have an insurance certificate proving you can cover all medical and hospital expenses you may incur whilst in France, including medical repatriation costs and expenses in the event of death.
- You are not allowed to do any paid work.

VLS-T Visiteur (Visa de Long Séjour Temporaire - Visiteur)

This visa is intended for those who have no intention of becoming residents in France. The VLS-T Visiteur visa can be valid for between 4 and 12 months.

Key Requirements

- A valid Passport with at least 3 months left on the date of your visa expiry.
- Healthcare insurance covering the duration of your stay.

Restrictions

- Non-renewable.

- You must prove adequate financial resources for the duration of your stay in France. This is equivalent to SMIC (minimum national wage) and in January 2025 was €1,426.30 net per month per adult. Any income must be stable and regular. You may use capital or a mix of capital and income to satisfy the financial resources requirement. Note: Child Tax Credit payments are not taken into account as they are paid to maintain children.
- You are not allowed to do any paid work.

VLS-TS Visiteur (Visa de Long Séjour Valant Titre de Séjour - Visiteur)

This visa is intended for those who plan to take up residency in France but do not plan, or need, to work. This visa is usually issued for 12 months and is renewable in France. It is the visa most often given to people who are fully retired and who have pensions or other independent financial means.

Key Requirements

- Valid Passport with at least 3 months left on the date of your visa expiry.
- Healthcare insurance covering the duration of your stay. The private health insurance must have a minimum coverage of €30,000 and include repatriation. You must maintain this insurance until you are accepted into the French healthcare system.

Restrictions

- You must prove adequate financial resources for the duration of your stay in France. income must be stable and regular. You may use capital or a mix of capital and income to satisfy the financial resources This is equivalent to SMIC (minimum national wage) and in January 2025 was €1,426.30 net per month per adult. Any requirement. **Note:** Child Tax Credit payments are not taken into account as they are paid to maintain children.
- You are not allowed to do any paid work.

A Word of Caution

Recently there have been a growing number of people in France on a VLS-TS Visiteur visa reporting that they have applied to change their visa/carte de sejour to one that allows them to work and that this is being refused.

In France the change from one visa/carte de sejour to a different type is called a change of status and the decision is usually made by the prefecture. There is no guarantee that a change of status will be allowed.

If you know you will not want to work and are planning a life of leisure living happily off your pension, savings, investments etc. then you should have no problems as the VLS-TS Visiteur visa is for people just like you.

However, some people have been advised by immigration experts to come on this visa whilst they look for paid work or renovate a property that they intend to run as a gite or chambre d'hote.

Evidence shows that some prefectures are not willing to allow a change of status from a visitor visa to a working or business visa. This may vary from prefecture to prefecture.

If you think you will want to work, start a business or be self-employed in the future, you should consider applying for a visa that allows you to do these activities.

Visas for Employment

I absolutely love it here. Never look back you only get one chance at life and you can do whatever makes you happy.

It is possible to move to France and work as an employed person. There are several visa options that allow you to do this and it is crucial that you apply for the correct one.

Please note that you cannot work in France without a visa that allows it and there is no such thing in France as a digital nomad visa.

Your employer can be a private employer (domestic work), a company or another type of organization.

In most cases the employer will have to apply for an autorisation de travail (work permit). There are several things the employer must do before they can offer a US passport holder a contract and there are penalties in place for any company that employs someone without the proper authorization.

An autorisation de travail is required no matter how long the employment contract will be for, unless it is one of the exemptions listed below.

If the application for the autorisation de travail is successful, you must attach the work permit to your visa and/or residence permit application.

However, if the annual gross salary is at least €43,243, you may qualify for one of the Passeport Talent visas and an autorisation de travail isn't required.

Feel free to look at all the different types of visa that allow you to work in France and make a short-list of the ones you need to focus on.

1. Short-Stay Work Visa (Visa de court séjour pour travailleur)

You'll need a short-stay work visa if you're coming to France for a job that lasts 90 days or less.

Note - you cannot work on the 90/180 days Schengen Visa waiver.

This type of visa is usually issued for temporary assignments, short-term contracts, or specific events (like artists or sports professionals coming for an event).

Key Requirements

- A valid job contract or assignment from a French employer (CDI or CDD)
- Authorization from the French labour authorities (usually handled by your employer) - autorisation de travail - unless exempt.
- Proof of sufficient financial means.

Restrictions

- You cannot extend this visa beyond 90 days.
- If you want to stay longer, you must apply for a long-stay work visa.

Exemption from autorisation de travail

Employers are exempt from applying for the autorisation de travail if the contract of employment is for 90 days or less AND concerns any of the following:

- Sporting, Cultural, Artistic or Science events
- Seminars or Trade Fairs
- The production and distribution of cinematographic or audio-visual performances or music publishing for artists and technicians directly involved in the product and realization
- roviding teaching activities, on an occasional basis, by visiting salaried teachers in France
- A modelling or artistic posing activity
- Personal service workers and domestic workers working in France during their private employer's stay in the country
- Audit and consulting in IT, management, finance, insurance, architecture, and engineering, under the terms of a service agreement or intra-company transfer agreement.

2. Seasonal Worker Visa (Visa travailleur saisonnier)

For those working in industries like agriculture, tourism, or hospitality on a seasonal basis.

Key Requirements

- A job contract with a French employer
- Autorisation de Travail (work permit)
- Proof that you will return to your home country after the season ends.

Restrictions

- Work is limited to six months per year.
- You cannot switch to a permanent contract from this visa.

3. VLS-TS Salarié

This is the standard work visa for employees with a job offer from a French company that doesn't qualify for one of the Passeport Talent visas.

Please note you cannot work as a salaried employee and run your own business at the same time. This is not allowed. You must choose whether you will get your income from an employment contract or a self-employed activity.

You need a different visa for a self-employed activity.

Key Requirements

- A valid work contract with a French employer
- Authorization from the French labor authorities - autorisation de travail
- A minimum salary that meets French regulations. This must be the current SMIC or more. (SMIC is the French minimum wage and is currently €1801.80 gross per month).
- Private Medical Insurance which must be maintained until you apply for, and are accepted into, the French Health system
- Needs validating (online) within 3 months of arrival. A validated visa is equivalent to a Titre de Séjour (Residence Permit).

- You can only work for the employer who sponsored your visa. (ie. obtained your autorisation de travail)

Restrictions

- Typically issued for one year but renewable.
- Family members do not automatically get work rights.

4. Passeport Talent : Carte de Séjour Pluriannuelle d'un Etranger en France (Talent Passport)

This visa (it's actually a residence permit) is designed for skilled professionals, entrepreneurs, and investors who intend to stay more than 12 months.

If you plan to stay less than 12 months, you apply for a VLS-TS Passeport Talent which needs to be validated online.

These visas do not require an employer to apply for an autorisation de travail.

There are several types of Passeport Talent, each with its own eligibility criteria (often qualifications and/or salary related). They also have some advantages over other types of visa.

- Valid for up to 4 years
- Allows more job flexibility than a VLS-TS Salarié
- Family members can also get residence permits and work rights.

I have listed the various types of Passeport Talent visas below and the key eligibility criteria for each one.

Talent Passport - Qualified Employee (Passeport Talent - Salarié Qualifié)

- You have studied in France and obtained a Master's Degree or its equivalent.
- You have an employment contract of more than 3 months that provides for annual gross earnings equal to or greater than €43,243 (this figure is correct as at January 2025).

Talent Passport - Recruitment in an Innovative Company (Passeport Talent - Entreprise Innovante)

- You have been recruited by an innovative young company or a company recognized as innovative by the Ministry of Economy
- Your duties are directly related to the research and development project of this company
- You have an employment contract that provides for gross annual earnings equal to or greater than €43,243 (this figure is correct as at January 2025).

Talent Passport - EU Blue Card (Passeport Talent - Carte Bleue Européenne)

- You must have a diploma with at least 3 years of higher education or 5 years of professional experience at a comparable level
- You need an employment contract for at least 1 year. You are getting a gross annual salary of at least €53,836.50 (this figure is correct as at January 2025).

Talent Passport - Employee on Assignment (Passeport Talent - Salarié en Mission)

- You are an employee of a foreign company and you are transferred to part of the same company or group in France
- You have a minimum of 3 months with the company abroad at a senior level
- You have an employment contract with the company that employs you in France. Your contract of employment must be with the company in France, not the company abroad. This means your conditions of employment may change to follow French labour laws.
- You receive a gross annual remuneration of at least €38,918.88 (this figure is correct as at January 2025)

Talent Passport - Researcher (Passeport Talent - Chercheur)

- You have a degree at masters level or above
- You are coming to France to conduct research or provide university-level education
- You have a hosting agreement signed with an approved public or private organization with a research or higher education mission. The agreement must indicate that you are a researcher and the purpose and duration of your stay in France.

Talent Passport - Social agent - all commercial activities related to the mandate (Passeport Talent - Mandataire Social)

- Your appointment as a legal representative of an establishment or company established in France.

- You have an employment contract of more than 3 months in an establishment or business of the same group
- Your annual gross earnings are greater than or equal to €64,864.80 (this figure is correct as at January 2025)

Talent Passport - Artistic and Cultural Profession (Passeport Talent - Profession Artistique et Culturelle)

- You are a performer or author of a literary or artistic work
- At least 51% of your required financial resources must come from your artistic or cultural activity. This should be at least €1,261.26 per month gross (this figure is correct as at January 2025).
- For income related to the planned activity in France you also need contract(s) of engagement that show a total duration of at least 3 months, over a maximum period of 12 months and a Cerfa 15617 completed by the employer.

5. Intra-Company Transfer Visa - VLS-TS ICT seconded employee (Salarié Détaché ICT)

If your company is transferring you from a branch outside France to a French office, this is the visa you'll need.

This type of visa is valid for 3 years. If the secondment is for less than 1 year you will be given a VLS-TS - Intra-company transfer (Salarié détaché ICT)

Key Requirements

- At least six months seniority in the group to which your company belongs.
- An employment contract with the home company sending you to work as a senior manager or expert in France. No employment contract is entered into with the host company in France.
- Your home company and the host company must belong to the same group.
- Your gross annual salary must be at least equivalent to legal and conventional minimums in France.

Restrictions

- You must stay with the same employer during your assignment.
- This visa is usually valid for 1-3 years and is non-renewable.

Another way of coming to France and earning money is to set up a business or register as self-employed.

This is the subject of our next chapter so if this is part of your plan, read on.

Visas for Self-Employment/Setting Up a Business

> Do you have tons of patience? Because basic things take forever.

There are lots of barriers that prevent companies from employing people from the US, including things like: the language barrier, the need for the employer to apply for a work permit and the fact that companies have to pay extra tax if they employ a foreign worker. There are a few exceptions to this.

The other option is to set up a business or become self-employed. In reality, these two things are very similar and whether you end up being self-employed or running a business depends on the structure you choose when you register your business activity.

France has some strict rules when it comes to running a business and it may seem complicated at first.

Things you may be thinking about doing that are likely to fall into the 'create a business' category include:

- Working as self-employed
- Freelancing
- Running a gite or chambre d'hote
- Online selling
- Working remotely for a company based outside of France
- Selling your hand-made craft items at craft fairs or on local markets.

All of these activities require you to have the correct visa and register your business activity in France. You will be given a SIRET/SIREN number.

One thing to note is that some professions in France are designated 'regulated' and require specific qualifications before you are allowed to do that activity.

Not all American qualifications are accepted in the EU so it is best to check if your profession is regulated and, if it is, whether your qualifications are accepted.

This is a good place to start:

https://www.france-education-international.fr/expertises/enic-naric?langue=en

A citizen of a third national country (including the US) who wants to undertake a regulated liberal activity in France, must apply for recognition of their professional qualifications and/or professional experience.

France offers several visa options depending on the nature of your work and your long-term plans.

However, before applying for your visa, if you want to create a retail, craft/artisanal or manufacturing activity you should develop a 3 year business plan and obtain an un avis favorable de l'administration - this will look at the economic viability of your proposed business - in other words, will your business plans realistically make a profit that is sustainable long-term.

You apply online here:

https://administration-etrangers-en-france.interieur.gouv.fr/particuliers/#/

Choose the option '*Demander une autorisation de travail*'

For activities falling under Profession libérales (regulated or unregulated) the avis favorable is not required but you will still have to present a business plan at your TLS appointment.

France offers several visa options depending on the nature of your work and your long-term plans.

1. Visa de Long Séjour valant Titre de Séjour (VLS-TS) Entrepreneur/Profession Libérale (VLS-TS Entrepreneur/Profession Libérale)

This is the most common visa for people who want to set up a business in France and who are not eligible for one of the Talent Passport visas.

Who is it for?

- People starting their own business in any sector
- Freelancers offering services in France
- Self-employed professionals such as consultants, artists, or tradespeople.

Key Requirements

- A well-prepared 3 year business plan demonstrating the business will make the minimum required income and that the business will be sustainable and profitable.

- Proof of sufficient financial resources to support yourself until your business becomes profitable (this must be included in your business plan). This can be savings but cannot be 401K or IRA unless the money is immediately available to you.
- Registration of your business with the appropriate French authority. This should be done soon after your arrival in France
- A clean criminal record.

You must validate the visa online within 15 days of arrival in France (some official Government sites also say 3 months!)

This visa is valid for one year and can be renewed, provided you continue to meet the requirements.

2. Passeport Talent – Créateur d'Entreprise (Talent Passport - Business Creation)

This visa is designed for people who plan to create or take over a business in France and invest significantly in the local economy.

The company may not yet exist or may have already been registered.

Who is it for?

- Business owners with a concrete project.
- People making an investment of at least €30,000 in their own business.
- Those taking over an existing French business.

Key Requirements

- A detailed business plan showing the financial viability and potential of your business.
- Proof of a financial investment of at least €30,000
- A qualification corresponding to a master's degree or equivalent, or at least five years' relevant professional experience
- You must obtain a letter approving your business plan. This is done online https://www.demarches-simplifiees.fr/commencer/passeport-talent-mention-creation-entreprise
- Financial resources corresponding to SMIC - €21,621.60 per year (correct in January 2025).

3. Passeport Talent – passeport talent - projet économique innovant (Talent Passport - Innovative Economic Project)

This is for people with an innovative business idea recognized by a French public body like Bpifrance or a startup incubator.

Key Requirements

- An innovative business project you want to develop in France
- Recognition of the project by a public-sector body
- Sufficient annual financial means corresponding to SMIC (€21,621.60 as of January 2025).

4. Passeport Talent - Investisseur économique (Talent Passport - Business Investor)

Who is it For?

This visa is for foreign investors wishing to settle in France to undertake a planned investment either:

- Personally
- Via a company they control
- Via a company in which they have at least a 30% shareholding.

Key Requirements

- You must be creating or protecting, or promising to create or protect, jobs within the four years following the investment.
- You are investing, or promising to invest, at least €300,000 in fixed tangible or intangible assets. Direct investments include share capital investments, reinvested earnings or loans between affiliated companies.

5. Passeport Talent - profession artistique et culturelle (Talent Passport - Artistic & Cultural Profession)

Who is it for?

This type of visa can be for employed or self-employed performers or authors of a literary or artistic work

- You are a performer or author of a literary or artistic work
- For income related to the planned activity in France you also need to show that 51% of your income is greater than or equal to €1,261.26 gross per month (this figure is correct as at January 2025) for the duration of your stay. This income needs to come from contract(s) with a gallery, artistic commissions etc.
- As well as income generated by your activity in France, your own resources, up to a maximum of 49% of the minimum required income, may be considered.

6. Passeport Talent - Renommée Nationale ou Internationale (Talent Passport - Renowned Persons, Nationally or Internationally)

Who is it for?

This visa is for individuals who are recognized for their exceptional achievements in arts, sciences, sports, education, or other fields including:

- Artists and Performers (e.g., musicians, filmmakers, writers, actors)
- Academics and Researchers
- High-Level Athletes
- Renowned Business Leaders
- Experts in Science and Technology

Key Requirements

- You must be able to provide evidence of your reputation and influence (eg. awards, published work, media coverage, or letters from recognized institutions.
- Prove your significant contribution to your field.
- Provide letters of recommendation from recognized institutions, employers, or industry professionals.
- Show proof of financial stability, such as contracts, sponsorships, or personal funds.
- Demonstrate a clear plan for your activities in France (e.g. exhibitions, research, business ventures).

This visa is typically granted for up to 4 years, with the possibility of renewal.

Restrictions

- You must primarily engage in the activity for which the visa was granted
- If employed, you cannot work outside the authorized professional scope specified in your application
- Changing professional fields may require modifying the residence permit
- Compliance with French tax and social security regulations is required

If you haven't yet worked out which visa is for you, maybe the next chapter will help.

The final chapter on the topic of types of visas covers visas for people who are looking to come to France to join a partner, spouse or family member already living in France or coming to France with them to take up residency.

Visas for Spouses, Partners and Family

> I love it here. The peace, the weather, the food. My only frustration is the red tape of getting set up with carte Vitale and other government processes. Its slow and prone to making annoying mistakes.

There are several different visas for partners, spouses and family moving to France.

The correct visa for you may depend on why you are moving to France and what visa your partner or spouse is applying for (if indeed they need a visa).
Below are the main categories of family and partner visas, along with their key requirements and restrictions.

1. VLS-TS Vie privée et familiale (VLS-TS Private and Family Life)

If you are married to a French citizen, you can apply for a long-stay spouse visa. This visa allows you to live, work, and study in France.

Requirements

- Marriage certificate proving a legal marriage with a French citizen. If you married outside of France you must register the marriage with the French Consulate in the country in which you got married.
- Proof of community of life with your French spouse and your intention to maintain it. This means things like both names on utility bills, joint bank accounts etc.
- A letter from the French spouse, dated and signed, describing the existence of the relationship before and after the marriage. He/She must express his/her desire for the foreign spouse to join him/her in France.

Restrictions

- Must validate visa online upon arrival
- Initially issued for one year, then renewable as a residence permit. This renewal can be for 2 years.
- After 3 years of proving a stable and regular stay on French territory, a 10-year resident card can be issued to spouses of French citizens.

2. VLS-TS Regroupement Familial (VLS-TS Family Reunification Visa)

This visa is for non-EU citizens, already legally residing in France, who wish to bring their spouse or children.

Requirement

- Proof of at least 18 months of legal residence in France - Temporary residence card of at least 1 year or multi-annual residence card
- Proof of sufficient and regular financial resources to support your family. Your resources must reach a certain net amount, which varies depending on the size of your family:

    1. 2 or 3 people: average gross monthly minimum wage (SMIC), i.e. on average €1,801.80 , over the 12 months preceding the request
    2. 4 or 5 people: on average €1,981.99 over the 12 months preceding the request
    3. 6 people or more: on average €2,162.16 over the 12 months preceding the request.

Your resources may come from income from salaried work or self-employment, from asset management, retirement pensions, etc.

Your spouse's resources are also taken into account, provided that they will continue to receive that income when they move to France.

- Adequately sized accommodation. You must be a tenant, an owner or an occupant of a house free of charge. The house must meet certain conditions, including size.

To see if the property you are living in is sufficient, you can check on this website. You just need your code postale (postcode in France)

https://www.service-public.fr/simulateur/calcul/zonage-abc

Restrictions

- Process can take several months for approval
- Family members cannot work until a residence permit is issued.

3. Spouses and Families of Talent Passport/ICT Visa Holders

If your partner holds a Passeport Talent visa or a VLS-TS (salarié détaché ICT (ICT seconded employee) you can obtain a residence permit without going through the family reunification procedure.

You benefit from the simplified procedure for an accompanying family.

This visa gives you the right to work or run a business.

The accompanying spouse will be issued with one of the following, depending on the visa held by the partner:

- Talent Passport - Family
- Intra-Company

Requirements

- Proof of marriage or civil partnership
- Proof of the Talent Passport/ ICT visa holder's legal status in France

Restrictions

- Valid for the same duration as the Talent Passport visa

4. Spouses and Partners of EU Citizens (Carte de Séjour – Membre de Famille UE/EEE/Suisse)

If your partner is an EU, EEA, or Swiss citizen residing in France, you can apply for a residence card as their family member.

For citizens of countries that benefit from the Schengen Visa Waiver (this includes US passport holders) you do not need a visa.

You can come to France to join your EU spouse or partner and then apply for a residence permit. You must apply for the residence permit within 3 months of arrival in France.

The residence permit in this case gives you the right to work in France.

Requirements

- Proof of relationship (marriage or civil partnership)
- Partner's proof of residence and financial means in France
- Proof of accommodation

5. Spouses and Family Members of Students

If you are moving to France as the spouse or dependent of a student, you can apply for a **Visa de Long Séjour – Vie Privée et Familiale**.

Requirements

- The student must have lived in France for at least 18 months. (Except Researchers on a Talent Passport)
- Proof of marriage or parent-child relationship
- Proof of financial means to support yourself
- Proof of suitable accommodation in France. To see if the property you are living in is sufficient, you can check on this website. You just need your code postale (postcode in France)

https://www.service-public.fr/simulateur/calcul/zonage-abc

Restrictions

- Does not automatically grant work rights (your employer must apply for a work permit for you)
- Valid for the duration of the student's visa

In the next few chapters, I will help you understand the application process and hopefully help you to get it done with the least amount of stress.

But first a quick word about 'digital nomads.'

Digital Nomads and Remote Working

> For me, the carte vitale is a significant issue. It's frustrating that I keep submitting the necessary documents, and after eight months, I received a letter stating they need my email to obtain the original documents. They already have my email and all of my documents.

More and more people are choosing to work as digital nomads.

It is estimated that 165,000 US citizens live and work abroad as digital nomads.

Globally, it's estimated that around 40 million people now earn a living through remote, location-independent work.

Many countries have created special digital nomad visas to welcome these workers - but France isn't one of them.

This has made the issue of living in France while working remotely for a company, or running a business based outside of France, a hot topic of debate.

Why is it so controversial?

Even visa experts and legal professionals can't seem to agree. Some argue that working (as in salaried employment) for a foreign employer while living in France is not allowed, while others believe it's fine.

If you bring up the topic in online forums, you'll likely get a mix of strong opinions on both sides.

While countries like Spain, Portugal and Italy have embraced digital nomads with dedicated visas, France has remained surprisingly silent.

The country does recognise remote work (or télétravail) and has updated its labour laws fairly recently to clarify employer and employee responsibilities, but at the moment (January 2025), this only applies to employees living in France and working for French companies.

However, official government sources provide little or no information on whether someone can legally live in France on a visa while working remotely for an overseas company.

For those hoping to fund their move to France this way, the lack of clear guidance can be frustrating and stressful.

I'll break down both sides of the argument, but the reality is that until France makes an official statement or introduces a digital nomad visa, there's no definitive answer on whether it's allowed.

Digital Nomad Working for a Company Outside France - Not Allowed

People who believe that working remotely in France for a foreign company is not allowed, point to one key fact: if your visa doesn't permit employment, self-employment, or starting a business, you have to sign a declaration stating that you won't engage in any professional activity.

French immigration law (the CESEDA Code) clearly states that certain visas and residence permits do not allow any kind of work.

These include:

- Visitor visa
- ICT intern
- Mobile ICT intern
- Private and family life visa (for the first 12 months)
- Intern visa
- Retired visa (for non-EU nationals receiving a French pension)

Because of this, supporters of the 'not allowed' stance argue that to work as a digital nomad in France, you must have a visa that explicitly allows self-employment or the creation of a business.

If digital nomads are not allowed on a Visitor Visa then these would be the current options:

1. Apply for a VLS-TS Entrepreneur/Profession Libérale visa. You can set up a business or as self-employed and invoice the company you work for (or own) for your work. You will pay social charges (cotisations) and tax in France.

2. Portage salarial - This is where you become an 'employee' of a third party company in France. It is an alternative to setting up a business or registering self-employed status. Essentially, the portage salarial company invoices your company for your work. The portage salarial takes care of your tax and cotisations payments in France. The portage salarial company also ensures that everything is within the French labour laws.

3. Your foreign company can register that they are employing someone living and working in France. They will have to pay employer and employee contributions which can prove expensive for the company (on average 42% of your gross salary). If you're worth it, they'll pay it!

Digital Nomad Working for a Company Outside France - Allowed

Recently there has been an increase in the number of immigration lawyers and other professional agencies arguing that it is possible to come to France as a digital nomad working for a foreign company on a 'Visitor' visa.

The argument from supporters of the allowed camp is that 'professional activity' only relates to business activity that involves French clients or invoicing French companies for work done. If you do not have any French clients or invoice any French companies then it doesn't apply.

Certainly the phrase 'professional activity' is not defined anywhere on the official documents (apart from to distinguish it from 'non-professional activity') and like most things legal, it can be open to interpretation.

What is true is that there are people who have been approved for a VLS-TS Visitor visa by the French Consulates in the US and their proof of adequate financial resources has been their income from their work for a company outside of France that they will continue to do in France. I personally know 3 people in this situation. It is also true that people have been refused a visa on this basis.

People applying for this visa still have to sign a statement saying they will not undertake professional activity whilst in France.

There is some talk that France is going to introduce a Digital Nomad Visa, possibly in 2026, but nothing has been confirmed at the time of writing.

Sorry - I realise that this doesn't really answer any questions you may have, or help you work out what is best for you. Let's just say it's complicated!

You may want to consult a lawyer or immigration specialist about this if it applies to your situation.

Visas for Running a Gite or Chambre d'Hotes

> Best decision I ever made. In my sixth year here, still working on being fluent in French but getting there.

If part of your dream in France is to run a gîte (self-catering holiday rental) or a chambre d'hôtes (bed and breakfast), then you're not alone.

Many US citizens love the idea of a slower-paced life in the French countryside, enjoying the local culture and welcoming guests.

However, before you start making the beds and serving croissants on the terrace, there are a few administrative procedures and rules you need to be aware of, and plan for.

The Rules for Gites and Chambre d'Hotes

Chambre D'Hotes: The description '*Chambre D'Hotes*' is regulated. The rental activity must take place at the home of the owner and the owner must host the guests in person (this cannot be delegated to another person, even when you go on holiday).
There are requirements that must be included in the service offered:

- A furnished room with linen provided. The minimum size of each room must be 9 m² (excluding toilets), with a ceiling height of at least 2.20 m
- Room temperature can be controlled separately to keep a minimum temperature of 19°C
- The room has access to a toilet and a bathroom with a washbasin, shower or bath. These don't have to be exclusive or 'en suite'
- Breakfast is included with each night's stay
- The chambre d'hotes follows health, safety and sanitary regulations
- The maximum number of letting rooms is five, accommodating up to 15 people.

Gîte: The official term is '*Meublés de tourisme*'

A gite can be located on the owner's property (must be separated from the owner's accommodation but can be attached so long as it has its own private entrance) or be away from the owner's main residence.

You can delegate the running of the gîte to someone else - you don't have to do it yourself.

You cannot rent your accommodation to the same client for more than 90 consecutive days per calendar year.

Getting Permission

The first thing to know is that you need permission from the Maire to run a gite or chambre d'hotes.

Be aware that the Maire can refuse if he believes that the level of tourism in the area can't support another one. With 2500 new gites or chambre d'hotes being created every year, some areas have become saturated.

If you get permission, you will then have to do a bit of form filling (the French love their forms)!
The need for permission from the Maire can mean that things have to be done in rather a strange order with regard to getting your visa, getting permission and getting the gite or chambre d'hotes up and running.

If you are property hunting, you could ask at the Mairie if the running of a gite or chambre d'hotes would be allowed in that commune, but any reply is not binding until you have received formal permission and signed the declaration.

If you have already bought a property you still need formal permission and will have to sign the declaration. If this is refused, then you will have to change your plans.

This means that you need to sort out the permission before you apply for a visa, as you may end up with the wrong type of visa.

Visa

This is where things can become complicated, which is why you have to be clear about your plans before applying for your visa.

You may hear the terms **LMP** (loueur en meublé professionnel) and **LMNP** (loueur en meublé non professionnel) being referred to in discussions about visas for running gites and chambre d'hôtes.

Many people mistakenly think that you only have to have a business visa (VLS-TS entrepreneur/profession libérale) if you are running an LMP.

This is not true - these terms are actually about how much tax you pay, not which visa you need.
If the gîte is not the source of your main income (you work as a salaried employee or have another business or are self-employed), then your gîte would count as non-professional.   The annual revenue from your gite under a non-professional registration must be less than 23,000 euros.

If you are running the gîte as a full-time business, all year round, it counts as your professional activity. For this an annual income of more than €23,000 is expected and this income needs to be greater than any other income generating activity in your household.

So having cleared up that common confusion let's now take a look at which visa you should get that will allow you to achieve your goal of becoming a gite or chambre d'hotes host.

There are two main things to consider before applying for your visa:

- Will you be up and running as a gite or chambre d'hotes immediately or will you be doing renovations etc first?
- Will this be your main activity to earn income?

Up & Running Immediately

If you plan to hit the ground running, then you will need a visa that allows you to set up a business.

This is usually the VLS-TS entrepreneur/profession libérale. (Other business visas do exist - take a look at the Talent Passport visas to see if any of them better suit your situation).

To be given the VLS-TS entrepreneur/profession libérale visa you will need to show:

- Your gite/chambre d'hotes business is viable, sustainable and profitable. You will need to submit a 3 year business plan. If the property you have bought has already been running as a gite complex or chambre d'hotes you can use their records and accounts to strengthen your case.

- It will create the minimum financial requirement for the visa (currently €23,000 per year / January 2025).
- All your income must come from the business. The exception to this is your first year when it is accepted that you can supplement your income from the business with other passive income (eg. pension, investments, dividends). You will need to reflect this in your business plan.
- You have premises from which to run your business - perhaps obvious for a gite or chambre d'hotes business - but it does mean you will have to complete on a property before submitting your visa application.
- You do not need to have private health insurance if you have a VLS-TS entrepreneur/profession libérale visa. When you register your business in France it automatically triggers the process for entry into the French healthcare system and you are covered from day one. You may however end up paying for health treatment upfront until you get your attestation des droits but you will be able to claim this back.
- You will be subject to a French language test and possibly compulsory lessons, the 4 day Civic Course and a medical.

Renovating or Property Searching

If you plan to move to France and renovate a property you already own or rent, or spend time in France searching for a suitable property to buy or rent, then you may be better off applying for a VLS-TS Visiteur Visa or the VLS-T Visiteur visa.

This has advantages and disadvantages:

- You won't have to go through the more complicated process of applying for a business visa until you are ready to start running the business.
- You will need to be financially independent whilst you do this (have funds equivalent or higher than the minimum national wage (SMIC)
- You will need to apply for a change of status when your visa/carte de sejour is due for renewal (VLS-TS visa only) This is not guaranteed to be granted. More and more US expats report that they have been refused a change of status from visiteur to entrepreneur/profession libérale.
- You will still have to submit a business plan for a change of status.
- If you opt for a VLS-TS Visiteur visa you will need to have private health insurance until you can enter the French health system.
- If you opt for the VLS-T visa you cannot renew it and you have to leave France before or on the expiry date. You would then have to apply for a new visa from the US. However, this may be a better option to avoid the refusals mentioned above.

At the time of writing (January 2025) I recommend getting a visa that allows you to run a gite or a chambre d'hotes from the outset, rather than a VLS-TS Visiteur visa.

It may be possible to change status from visiteur to entrepreneur/profession liberale but there is a big risk involved. You are the only one who can determine your attitude to such a risk.

Using an agency, maintenance company etc. to manage your gite (This only applies to gites and is not possible for Chambre d'hotes)

You can come on a VLS-TS visiteur visa and have a gite business so long as you have nothing to do with that gite business.

This means you cannot do any marketing, changeovers, gardening or building maintenance (this is not an exhaustive list). It all has to be outsourced.

Registering Your Business

If you're running a chambre d'hôtes or gîte as a business, you must register it with the French authorities.

You can do this online

https://www.inpi.fr/formalites-entreprises/creer-son-entreprise/

Final Thoughts

Running a gîte or chambre d'hôtes in France can be a rewarding experience, but it does come with legal and financial responsibilities.

Ensuring you have the right visa is a good place to start.

Qualifications

There will be a bit of a cultural shock. It is the point actually. Do you want to experience something new in your life? Do you want to embrace the difficulty? If not, if you come with a resisting mind, it is going to be a struggle.

If you're moving to France for work or business, it is important to understand that France has regulated and unregulated professions.

You may need to go through a recognition process or even additional training to do certain jobs.

This chapter will help you understand how US qualifications are (or aren't) recognized in France, particularly for regulated professions.

Regulated vs. Non-Regulated Professions

There are more than 250 professions that are regulated in France.

This means that anyone wishing to do one of these professions in France requires specific qualifications and/or authorization to practice in France. Examples include doctors, lawyers, architects, and teachers.

If your profession is regulated, you'll need to get formal recognition before you can work.

Regulated professions often have the requirement that you are registered or licensed by a professional body in addition to qualifications.

In 2023, three groups of regulated professions libérales were defined:

- health professions (doctor, nurse, dentist, etc.);
- the legal or judicial professions (lawyer, judicial representative, etc.);
- technical and living environment professions (includes other regulated professions libérales).

Please note that there is no official definitive list of regulated professions but you can consult a directory of some regulated professions here

https://www.inpi.fr/en/directory-of-regulated-professions-activities

This site has useful fact sheets for many professions - some may surprise you!

A non-regulated profession does not require official recognition, meaning employers can decide whether your US qualification is sufficient. IT, business services and creative sector jobs fall into this category.

Additionally, you can set up a business or register as self-employed without having to have your qualifications or experience assessed if you are planning to work in one of the unregulated professions.

However, when you are applying for a visa that allows you to set up a business or register as self-employed, the consulate may want to know what experience or qualifications you have that will allow you to run a profitable and sustainable business.

Qualification Recognition

Depending on your profession, you may still be able to get your qualifications recognized through a formal process.

There are two main types of recognition:

1. existing agreements or well-established processes.

2. Case-by-Case Recognition – Many professions require an application to a relev Automatic Recognition – Some professions benefit from ant French authority for assessment.

How to Get Your Qualifications recognized

If your profession is regulated, you will need to apply to the relevant French authority for recognition. The process usually involves:

- Submitting an application with proof of your US qualifications
- Providing details of your professional experience
- Possibly taking additional training or exams to meet French standards

Key Recognition Authorities for Regulated Professions

- Health and Medical Professions – The Ordre des Médecins (for doctors), Ordre des Infirmiers (for nurses etc)
- Legal Professions – The Conseil National des Barreaux (for lawyers)
- Teaching Professions – The Ministère de l'Éducation Nationale
- Engineering and Technical Fields – The Commission des Titres d'Ingénieur (CTI)
- Finance and Accounting – The Ordre des Experts-Comptables (for accountants)

Each organization has its own process, so it's best to check their website or contact them directly for specific requirements.

Diploma Recognition through ENIC-NARIC

If your profession is not regulated but you still want official confirmation that your qualification is equivalent to a French diploma, you can apply for a comparability statement from France Éducation International (ENIC-NARIC France).

This can help employers understand how your US qualifications fit into the French system.

https://www.france-education-international.fr/en/expertises/enic-naric

Do You Need Additional Training?

In some cases, US professionals may need extra training or certification to meet French standards. This depends on the profession and how different US qualifications are from their French equivalents.

Some regulated professions require passing a test or completing a short adaptation period.

Tips for a Smooth Recognition Process

- Start early – The recognition process can take several months.
- Gather all necessary documents – Diplomas, transcripts, and proof of work experience are often required.Get certified translations – Many authorities require official translations of documents into French.

- Check professional bodies – Your US professional organization may have advice on working in France.
- Consider alternative pathways – If recognition is difficult, look for roles that don't require formal validation.

Conclusion

Obviously qualification recognition can make your planned move to France a bit more complicated but many US professionals manage to have their qualifications recognized in France.

By understanding the process and preparing your application properly, you can successfully continue your career in France despite having a few small hurdles to jump over.

Whilst I have taken great care to ensure that the information in this book is correct, immigration law is always evolving.

Scan Here

Subscribe easily

Keep up to date with any changes in the law or procedures by subscribing to our exclusive 'Moving To France' club.

Only €1.99 per month or €20 per year.

https://worldseyebooks.com/b/JUnT4

We will update you by email about any changes in the law or procedures that might affect you, and you will have access to our monthly webinars with experts on all things France.

You get the emails, the webinars with experts and you can message me with any questions and you can CANCEL ANYTIME.

Just scan the QR code or go to the website and pay securely via STRIPE, a highly secure payment platform trusted by businesses worldwide.

The Application Process

> France is chaotic, beaureacratic, slow, and messy but it's also exquisitely beautiful, full of life, with really fascinating and kind people, so much culture, history and charm - tons of charm!

So, you've figured out which visa you need - great start!

Now it's time to begin your application.

Let me just begin by saying you WILL feel overwhelmed by the French paperwork (yes there's paperwork even though it's an online process to begin with) and the whole visa process. Just accept that this will happen and roll with it.

Plan to reward yourself when you have finished the application - you'll have worked hard and overcome some obstacles on the way. You'll deserve something nice!

I've broken it down into steps and you should do the same. Just focus on one step at a time and you'll get there in the end.

This is the website you need to go to to start the application process.

https://france-visas.gouv.fr/en/online-application

There is a choice of six languages including English - you'll see the place to change the language at the top of the webpage.

You will need to create an account before you can start your application or log in if you have already created an account.

You can apply up to 6 months before the planned dates of travel for a short-stay visa and 3 months for a long-stay visa. (Correct at the time of writing, January 2025).

Processing of the visa AFTER your appointment with TLS is usually around 15 working days but this can be longer depending on the time of year (Easter, Christmas, Summer holidays) or staff shortages.

Step 1: Gather Your Documents

First things first - every visa application requires a certain set of documents. While the exact paperwork varies depending on your visa type, here's a general checklist to get you started.

If you do this first you'll know early on if one or more of the required documents are missing and you'll have plenty of time to get them.

- A valid passport. This means a passport that's issued for 10 years and will still have at least three months left before it expires on the date you plan to leave France or when your visa runs out.
- If you are a legal resident in the US but not a US national you must also provide evidence that you are legally resident in the US. You need to provide a valid Green Card or US alien registration card that is valid for at least three months after your intended return date.
- A completed visa application form (found here)

https://france-visas.gouv.fr/en/online-application

- 2 (or 3) Passport-sized photos that meet French visa requirements. Strangely enough, different pages on the official France Visa website say different things. Some say two passport sized photos are required, others say three. My advice is to have 3 just in case! Just to warn you - I could write a book just about what photos are accepted and that meet the French Visa Requirements. I have written a guide about acceptable photos in a separate chapter so make sure you read that before ticking the 'photos' part of your checklist as done!
- Proof of why you're moving (job contract, school acceptance letter, proof of financial means, etc.)
- Proof of adequate funds (usually at least the minimum wage - SMIC - per person
- Proof of accommodation in France (rental contract, hotel booking, a certificate stamped by the Mairie if staying with family or friends).
- Proof of health insurance. There is a chapter on health insurance requirements so make sure you understand what type of insurance is accepted for visa applications before buying it.
- If you are applying for a visitor visa that doesn't allow work you must submit a handwritten letter promising you will not undertake work whilst you are in France. You may also submit a second letter outlining what you will be doing if not working. I recommend you do this even though it's optional.

Step 2: Apply Online

You need to go to the official visa application portal for France

https://france-visas.gouv.fr/en/online-application

You'll need to fill out the online application form.

You must print out your completed application form at this stage or at least save it to your computer to print out later. You will need to take this to your interview with TLS.

Submitting your application is not the end of the process.

Applying for a French visa also involves a face-to-face interview at a TLS Centre. These are the people who check you have submitted everything correctly and then pass it on to the French Consulate in Washington for a decision.

There are 10 TLS centres in the US - Atlanta, Boston, Chicago, Houston, Los Angeles, Miami, New York, San Francisco, Seattle, and Washington DC. (See full addresses at the end of this chapter).

Once you have submitted your online application you will be directed to book an appointment at the centre of your choice.

Getting an appointment at one of these centres is one of the most frustrating parts of the whole process. People often report being told there are no appointments available.

Note: If you don't book an appointment within 10-12 business days of completing the forms your account may be closed and you have to start again.

I know this seems unfair, as one of the reasons for not making an appointment is that there are no available appointments on the TLS website!

This means you have to be flexible (be prepared to travel to another centre), spend a frustrating amount of time checking for available appointments without logging on too often which will see you locked out of the website for hours or be more flexible about the time and date you are available to go to an appointment.

Another common problem seems to be getting locked out of the website.

If you have problems then please read the chapter on TLS - there are some things to do (or not to do) which may solve any problems you're having.

Step 3: Attend Your Visa Appointment

You will be required to pay for your visa and application at your appointment with TLS. There are 2 fees to pay: a fee for the visa and a service fee for TLS.

At your appointment, you'll need to:

- Submit your documents, including three passport-size photos that meet the required visa application standards. If the photos you've brought are rejected, you may be able to do them in the TLS centre. If you are missing copies of documents you may be able to have them printed at the TLS centre for a cost.
- Provide fingerprints (biometric data)
- Pay the visa application fee (amount depends on your visa type) and the service fee.

- Answer a few basic questions about your plans in France.

Top Tip: Bring printed copies of everything. You will need one copy of everything for each person applying for a visa. You will need to bring a printed copy of the application form and the required documents.

This is part of the frustrating French bureaucracy I warned you about. So deep breath…and get printing. You will also need to hand your passport over.

Step 4: Wait for Processing

Once you have had your appointment with TLS, the processing time is usually 15 working days, but this can be longer depending on the type of visa you have applied for and the time of year.

You can track your application status online. However, the online tracking system will not tell you if your application has been successful or not.

You will be sent a notification when your passport is ready to be collected or returned (if you paid extra for this option).

You will only know if your application has been successful once you get your passport back.

Step 5: Receive Your Visa

If, or when (let's be positive), your visa is approved, you'll get a sticker placed inside your passport.

Double-check all the details to make sure there are no mistakes.

Step 6: Travel to France!

You did it! Now, all that's left is to pack your bags and move to France. But remember - some long-stay visas require you to validate them once you arrive in France, so be sure to check whether this applies to you.

Depending on the visa you have received, you will have to leave France on or before the expiry date unless you have a renewable visa.

Up next: a deep dive into the required documents and how to make sure your application is strong and rejection-proof.

Here Comes the Paperwork!

Making Sure You Have the Correct Documents

Best decision I ever made!

Paperwork is at the heart of anything you want to do in France and applying for a visa is no exception.

If you don't have the right documents your application could be delayed or rejected.

In this chapter I'll walk you through exactly what you need.

Core Documents

No matter which visa you're applying for, you'll need these:

- A valid passport – Must be a 10-year passport with at least three months left on the date your visa expires. If it's close to expiring, renew it before applying. It must also have at least 2 blank pages.
- Completed visa application form – Found here

https://france-visas.gouv.fr/en/online-application

- 2 (or 3) x Passport-sized photos – Must meet French visa photo requirements (check dimensions and background rules!) and taken no more than 6 months ago. Strangely enough, different pages on the official France Visa website say different things. Some say 2 passport sized photos are required, others say 3. My advice is to have 3 just in case!
- Proof of why you're moving to France – This could be a job contract, school acceptance letter, proof of funds, or family connection. A letter (1 x A4) outlining your plans is also a good idea - the French consulate seems to expect this now even though the official sites say it is optional.

- Proof of accommodation – Rental agreement, hotel booking, or an official invitation from a host or proof of ownership of a property in France. Showing them a picture of your beautiful French home isn't good enough! You'll need recent (less than 3 months old) copies of utility bills in your name or the attestation from the notaire if you bought your property less than 3 months before.
- Medical insurance – You will need to have the following, depending on your visa type:

If you have a VLS-T or a VLS-TS valid for between 7 and 12 months you will need full private health insurance, that must include medical repatriation and expenses in the event of death. It must have a minimum coverage amount of €30,000 and cover emergency and/or hospital treatment and cover doctor consultations, specialist appointments and prescribed medication.

Make sure you get written confirmation that the insurance policy you choose covers you as a resident in France, not just as a traveler, and confirms you are entitled to a full refund if your visa application is rejected on the grounds that you don't have health insurance that meets the requirements for your visa

TLS recommends https://insurte.com/, but there are many other companies out there providing health insurance that meets the visa application requirements.

One I have seen recommended recently is https://europe-insurance.eu/

I haven't used it myself but it seems a lot cheaper than many policies I have seen. It says it is suitable for visas for France and it comes with a guarantee of a full refund if you don't get your visa because the insurance doesn't meet the requirements.

If you are applying for an VLS-TS entrepreneur/profession libérale visa you do not need private health insurance.

When you register your business it will automatically trigger the process to apply to be in the French healthcare system.

However this can take several months. You therefore need to consider how you will pay for any medical costs that you might have until you get your attestation des droits.

If you pay these expenses out of your own pocket you will be able to claim them back once you have the attestation so long as you have a receipt (called a feuille des soins). Otherwise, you may want to consider private health insurance.

Extra Documents Depending on Your Visa Type

Work Visa Applicants

- Work contract signed by your French employer.
- Proof your employer has obtained a work permit (autorisation de travail) for you.
- Qualifications or experience proof (if required). This will depend on the type of work you are doing and whether it is a regulated or protected profession. Please refer to the section on 'Qualifications' for more information.

- Business plan if you are applying for a VLS-TS Entrepreneur/Profession Liberale visa.
- The avis favorable if you are required to apply for one when applying for a VLS-TS Entrepreneur/Profession Liberale visa.

Student Visa Applicants

- Acceptance letter from a French school/university.
- Proof of financial support showing at least €615 per month. Accepted proof includes: bank account statements, a guarantor's letter, an invoice of funding from a loan agency/bank, a scholarship letter, or a grant statement from the sponsoring body.

Family Visa Applicants

- Marriage or birth certificates to prove your relationship.
- Proof that your sponsor in France can support you financially.
- A letter from your French spouse (if applicable) confirming that he/she wants you to join them.

Visitor Visa Applicants (not working in France) but resident

- Bank statements showing you have enough money to support yourself (usually around €1426 per month net per adult). This figure is correct as of January 2025.
- A letter explaining why you want to live in France without working and your plans.
- A separate letter promising not to undertake any work activity whilst in France.

Check, Check, and Check Again

1. **Double-check all documents** – Make sure names, dates, and details match across all paperwork.

   The French are very keen on all official documents having matching names. In the US you may go by a name that is not the given first name on your birth certificate. It's also common for people to have used their birth name on their birth certificate and marriage certificate but use a different name that they are known by for things like a driving licence, utility bills or even hotel reservations.

This can cause problems with your visa applications and it's not unknown for applications to be rejected because the names on the various required documents don't match. If this is the case for your documents, change them before you apply.

2. **Make copies of everything** – Bring at least one extra set of copies to your appointment.
3. **Submit clear and complete paperwork** – No blurry scans, missing pages, or handwritten alterations.
4. **Be ready to explain your case** – If asked, be prepared to clarify why you're moving and how you'll support yourself.

Trouble-Shooting TLS

> We moved to Béziers a little over 3 years ago and wouldn't change it for the world. We love it!

If you're a US passport holder seeking to visit France or move there, you will have to apply for your visa through TLS.

They are the official partner responsible for managing visa applications.(It used to be VFS Global but this changed to TLS on 18th April 2025).

Understanding their role, the application process, common challenges, and strategies to overcome them can significantly ease your journey.

I'll give you a heads up before we continue - dealing with TLS can be a bitter sweet experience.

Who is TLS?

In the US, TLS operates 10 visa application centres on behalf of the French Consulate - Atlanta, Boston, Chicago, Houston, Los Angeles, Miami, New York, San Francisco, Seattle, and Washington DC.

They are the people who are responsible for:

- **Appointment Scheduling**: Setting up the in-person appointments for visa applicants.
- **Document Verification**: Ensuring all necessary documents are correctly submitted.
- **Biometric Data Collection**: Capturing fingerprints and photographs as part of the visa requirements.
- **Application Tracking**: Providing applicants with the ability to monitor the status of their visa applications.

They are not the place to seek advice about what is and isn't allowed. Their role is purely administrative and although you may find their staff will give some advice if you ask, they are not trained to do this and the advice they give may be wrong.

Accessing TLS Services

Applications can only be made from locations that appear to be from the US (this can be a problem if you use security software to hide your location).

Any mobile number you are required to give must be a US mobile phone number. You should use the same number anytime you contact TLS, therefore you must be confident you will have access to this phone number throughout the whole process.

Do not use the '+' sign in front of 1.

To begin your visa application process, you must start your visa application online

https://france-visas.gouv.fr/en/online-application.

Once you have completed this first part of the application you will be directed to the TLS website, where you can create an account, complete your application, and schedule an appointment at one of their US centers.

Common Challenges Encountered

While many applicants successfully navigate the TLS system, some have reported challenges, including:

1. **Website Navigation Difficulties**: You may find the website difficult to follow. For example, links are not always clearly marked, requiring applicants to hunt for the correct navigation.
2. **Account Registration Issues**: You may face problems when registering a new account, such as the system not recognising your email address or indicating you are already logged in from another device.
3. **One-Time Passcode (OTP) Failures**: During the application process, TLS sends an OTP to verify your identity. There have been instances where these codes are not received, delaying the progress of your application.
4. **Access Restrictions Due to Multiple Logins**: You might find yourself blocked after attempting to log in multiple times within a short period.
5. **Delay in new Information showing on your account**: You may experience delays of several days for information you submitted on the France-Visas page to be recognized by TLS, leading to a delay in being able to schedule an appointment

Strategies to Overcome These Challenges

If you are faced with any of these problems here are some things you can try:

- Use a US-Based IP Address: Make sure you are connecting to the TLS website from within the US,

as the system has geo-location validation and may restrict access from other countries.
- Accurate Mobile Number Entry: Enter your US mobile number in the correct format (without the '+' sign but using 001) as this is how TLS contacts you with a one time passcode and other communications.
- Limit Login Attempts: Avoid lots of login attempts in a short amount of time. Wait before trying again or contact TLS for assistance.
- Prepare Documentation Thoroughly: Ensure all your supporting documents are organised and correctly formatted before your appointment.
- Apply Well in Advance: Start your application early, especially during peak periods. The earliest you can begin the application process is 180 days before your intended arrival in France for a short-stay visa and 3 months before your intended date of travel for a long-stay visa.

Things to Know that will frustrate you

1. You can't check what new appointments are available without cancelling your first one, so try and be sure you can attend any appointment you make.
2. You can't phone to cancel an appointment and/or ask for a new one.
3. Don't be tempted to refresh your page if things seem slow - this can lead to being blocked for several hours. Always use the navigation keys.
4. If you want to attend the appointment with your spouse/partner/family you are advised to set up a group for all the applications. However, from what I hear, there are often less appointments available to choose from than if you do single applications.

5. Logging in too many times in the same day can get you blocked for the rest of the day.

Tips to help smooth the process

- Screenshot everything, particularly if you have asked for advice or reporting technical issues. It's one of those things that could be 'good to have' at some point.
- Make sure you have your TLS application reference number handy. I suggest putting it on a post-it note (showing my age) in your office, in your kitchen, on your wallet etc. or store it in your phone as a 'note' or similar.

Appointments

One of the biggest frustrations that people have with TLS is the lack of available appointments.

Some people are reporting that it took 6 weeks to get an appointment.

You could try choosing another centre for your appointment if you don't mind travelling a bit further.

Other people report that they release appointments in 4 week blocks between 6.30am and 8.30am.

Conclusion

While the visa application process through TLS may present certain challenges, being informed and prepared can significantly smooth your experience.

By understanding common issues and implementing the suggested strategies, you can navigate the process more effectively, bringing you one step closer to your journey to France.

Contact Details for TLS

+1 305 602 5861 From Monday to Friday between 8:30 a.m. and 3:30 p.m

Contact Addresses for TLS Centers

Atlanta
Spaces - Suite 242
3372 Peachtree Road
2nd Floor
Atlanta, GA 30326

Boston
Regus - Suite 1619
101 Federal Street
16th Floor
Boston, MA 02110

Chicago
Expansive - Suite 100B
405 W Superior St.
1st Floor
Chicago, IL 60654

Houston
Expansive - Suite 200E
3120 Southwest Freeway
2nd Floor
Houston, TX 77098

Los Angeles
Spaces City National Plaza - Suite 1840
515 South Flower Street
18th Floor
Los Angeles, CA 90071

Miami
Expansive - Suite 400A
2125 Biscayne Blvd
4th Floor
Miami, FL 33137

New York
Spaces - Suite 705
Met Tower
142 W 57th St.
7th Floor
New York, NY 10019

San Francisco
Regus - Suite 1033
315 Montgomery St.
10th Floor
San Francisco, CA 94104

Seattle
Regus Seattle City - Suite 2225
1420 Fifth Avenue
4th Floor
Seattle, WA 98101

Washington DC
1899 L St. NW
5th Floor
Washington, DC, 20036

Photograph Requirements

> It was not easy for the first year or so because it takes time to meet people and make friends. And I did miss those comforts of home in the US but I feel very anchored here and happy.

When applying for a French visa from the US, one of the key requirements is providing the correct type of photographs.

If your photographs don't meet the specific requirements when you go to your appointment at TLS, you will have to have them redone immediately before they can process your application.

Your photos must be less than 6 months old and show an accurate likeness on the day your application is submitted.

The photos must also be printed on high quality paper at a high resolution.

To help you get it right the first time, let's go through the key requirements, including size, background, and facial features and expressions.

Photo Size Requirements

French visa photos must follow specific size regulations. The official requirement is:

- Size: 35mm by 45mm.
- The face should take up between 70% and 80% of the image, from your head to the top of your shoulders.

Background Requirements

France has strict rules about this: Plain, light-coloured background (light grey, cream, or blue is acceptable).

- No patterns or shadows – ensure the lighting is even (no flash flares) and there are no distractions.
- No objects or people in the background – it must be completely clear.
- Have appropriate brightness and contrast

Facial Features and Expression

France requires visa photos to clearly show your natural facial features. Here's what you need to keep in mind:

- You must be looking directly at the camera
- Your skin tones must be natural
- Face fully visible – The photos must show both edges of your face
- Show your eyes open and visible - no hair covering your eyes or part of your face.
- Neutral expression – no smiling, frowning, or raising eyebrows
- Mouth closed – no teeth should be visible.
- No red eye.

If you wear glasses

- Thin frames only – thick frames can obscure your eyes
- Make sure the frames do not cover any part of your eyes
- No reflections or glare – this is a common reason for photo rejection
- No tinted lenses or sunglasses – only clear lenses are allowed. You must be able to see your eyes fully. If in doubt, remove your glasses.

For religious or medical head coverings

- Head coverings are not allowed unless they are for religious reasons
- The forehead, chin, and edges of the face must be fully visible
- The material should not cast shadows on your face.

Common Mistakes to Avoid

Even small mistakes can lead to having to have the photos redone. Here are some common errors:

- Incorrect size – always stick to 35mm x 45mm
- Dark or patterned backgrounds – only use plain light colours
- Smiling or tilting your head – maintain a neutral, straight-on look
- Glasses with reflections – remove them if necessary
- Poor quality images – photos must be clear, in focus, and not pixelated.

Summary

- Photos must just be of you (no one else can be in the photo)
- Photos cannot show anything in the background (chair back, toys, books etc)
- You must be looking directly at the camera
- You must have a neutral expression
- Your mouth must be closed.

There's a helpful official guide to help you take photographs for your visa application that conform to the requirements https://france-visas.gouv.fr/documents/d/france-visas/iso_iec_fv_visa_photograph_requirements_en

Health Insurance

I do love my life here. Slower, calmer, there's a quality of life here that I find very comforting.

It is essential that anyone who is a US passport holder (without dual nationality of an EU country) has health insurance to get their visa. (Obviously if you have dual nationality and have an EU passport you won't need a visa). You will be asked to prove it at your interview with TLS.

In this chapter, I'll explain what you need, and your options for getting insured.

Health Insurance Requirements by Visa Type

Depending on your reason for moving to France, the health insurance requirements will vary.

Work Visas

If you're moving to France for a job, your employer will typically register you for the French social security system (Sécurité Sociale), giving you immediate access to public healthcare.

If you are moving to France and becoming self-employed or setting up a business, the process for entry into the French health system is triggered by the registration of your self-employment or business on the Inpi website.

Retiree and Non-Working Visas

If you're moving to France without a job (such as retirees or those on long-stay visitor visas), you won't have automatic access to public healthcare.

You must provide proof of comprehensive private health insurance covering all medical expenses, including hospitalization. The insurance should give a minimum coverage of €30,000 and include medical repatriation to the US. It must also cover emergency and routine hospital visits, visits to a doctor and appointments with specialists.

TLS recommend https://insurte.com/ - it is guaranteed to meet the health insurance requirements for a visa.

https://europe-insurance.eu/ - recently I have seen a few recommendations for this company. They appear cheaper than a lot of other policies and they also guarantee that it will meet the health insurance requirements for a visa or they will give you a full refund.

Of course there are lots of other copmpanies offering visa compliant health insurance so shop around.

After three months of legal residence, you may apply to PUMA for access to the state healthcare system, but it can take several months to process and you must maintain your private health insurance until you have received notification that you have been accepted.

Student Visas

Students moving to France for higher education are required to have health insurance.
If you're under 28 and enroling in a French university, you may be eligible for student social security, which gives access to state healthcare.

If you're not eligible, you must arrange private health insurance before your visa is approved.

Family and Partner Visas

If you're moving to France to join a spouse or family member, your access to healthcare will depend on their status.

If your spouse is employed in France, you may be added to their social security and healthcare coverage. Until this happens, you'll need private health insurance to meet visa requirements.

Choosing the Right Health Insurance

When selecting a health insurance policy for your visa, make sure it meets these key criteria:

- Covers all medical expenses including emergency and routine hospitalization
- Coverage of a minimum of €30,000 per person per year
- Includes medical repatriation coverage
- Valid for the entire duration of your visa.

Conclusion

Having the right health insurance is a key step in securing your visa.

While the French healthcare system is excellent, you may need private insurance initially.

It is also a good option for those who don't require it for their visa application (eg. entrepreneur/profession libérale) but will have to wait until they are fully in the French healthcare system which can take several months.

Understanding your options will help you stay covered and avoid any issues with your visa application.

To learn more about the French healthcare system take a look at the chapter entitled 'The French Healthcare System for New Residents'.

How To Write a Covering Letter

> Best decision we ever made. Blown away every day, even after 2 years. Love it here.

When applying for a visa to visit or move to France, you may be asked to provide a covering letter.

Although it is optional, I highly recommend you do one.

This letter is your opportunity to explain why you want to visit or move to France and how you meet the visa requirements.

It should help the French authorities understand your plans and your ability to support yourself while in the country.

Most visa applications are refused for one of two reasons:

- Insufficient proof of financial resources
- Incomplete or unreliable information about the purpose and conditions of your stay

The letter is your opportunity to address those questions before your application is refused.

What to Include in Your Letter

Don't forget to be clear about your plans in your letter.

It should refer to the specific visa you are applying for and how you meet the criteria for that specific visa, including how you will meet the financial requirements.

Here's what to include:

1.Introduction

- Your full name, nationality, and passport number.
- The type of visa you are applying for.
- A brief mention of your motivation for moving to or visiting France.

2. Why You Want to Visit or Move to France

- Explain why you have chosen France over other countries.
- Mention any personal, professional, or academic reasons.
- Highlight previous visits to France or any connection you have to the country.

3. Your Plans in France

- Describe what you will be doing in France (tourism, visiting family, studying, working, setting up a business, retiring, etc.).
- Mention where you plan to live.

4. Your Financial Situation

- Explain how you will support yourself financially (savings, salary, sponsorship, pension, etc. Note - you cannot include your 401K or IRA unless the money is immediately available to you).

5. Commitment to French Laws and Visa Conditions

- Confirm that you understand and will comply with visa regulations.
- Mention how you plan to integrate into French society, such as learning the language or contributing to the economy.

6. Conclusion

- Express gratitude for considering your application.
- Offer to provide additional documents if needed.
- End with a polite closing and your signature. You could use this French phrase which might (or might not) help your case: 'Je vous prie d'accepter, (Madame, Monsieur, ou Mademoiselle), l'expression de mes sincères salutations'.

Mistakes to Avoid

To make a good impression, avoid these common mistakes:

- Being too vague – Clearly outline your plans and financial situation.
- Making it too long – Stick to one page and certainly no more than one and a half pages.
- Using informal language – Keep it polite, professional, and well-structured.
- Not tailoring it to your visa type – Make sure the letter directly supports your visa application.
- Ignoring formatting – Use short paragraphs and a formal letter layout.

Final Tips

- Write in English or French – A letter in English is acceptable but if you are fluent in French, why not submit it in French?
- Be honest – Any false information can lead to rejection
- Proofread – Spelling and grammar mistakes can make a bad impression

A well-crafted letter can strengthen your application and show the authorities that you have a clear, well-prepared plan for your time in France.

Whilst I have taken great care to ensure that the information in this book is correct, immigration law is always evolving.

Scan Here

Subscribe easily

Keep up to date with any changes in the law or procedures by subscribing to our exclusive 'Moving To France' club.

Only €1.99 per month or €20 per year.

https://worldseyebooks.com/b/JUnT4

We will update you by email about any changes in the law or procedures that might affect you, and you will have access to our monthly webinars with experts on all things France.

You get the emails, the webinars with experts and you can message me with any questions and you can CANCEL ANYTIME.

Just scan the QR code or go to the website and pay securely via STRIPE, a highly secure payment platform trusted by businesses worldwide.

How To Handle Delays and Rejections

> Wish I wouldn't have waited so long. Love my life here. So much healthier and happier.

So, you've done everything by the book, submitted your visa application, and now... you wait.

But what happens if things don't go smoothly? Don't panic - just breathe!

Dealing with Delays

Visa processing times can feel unpredictable, and as your travel date gets closer you might start to panic. Here's what you can do if your application is taking longer than expected:

- Check the estimated processing time – Every visa type has an average processing time listed on the France-Visas website. For a VLS-TS or VLS-T visa the average processing time is 15 working days.
- Track your application – You can track your application online. At your interview TLS will have given you a tracking number.
- Be patient – Some delays are normal, especially during busy periods like summer or the start of the school year.
- Follow up if needed – If your application is taking much longer than expected, you can contact the consulate or TLS for an update.

What to Do If Your Visa is Rejected

Rejections do happen. There are some common reasons for a visa application to be refused. Some of those reasons are:

- Your application form was incomplete or incorrect

- You didn't leave France when the 90 days allowed by the Schengen Visa waiver had expired, or overstayed a previous visa.
- You didn't give enough proof of financial resources. Either you didn't provide bank statements and other documents or those that you did submit don't back up your claim that you have the required minimum amount for the full duration of your stay.
- You didn't provide proof that you would return to your home country when your visa expires. If the consulate doesn't believe you will leave France on or before the visa expiry date they will reject the visa application. This is mainly for non-renewable visas.
- You didn't have health insurance that met the visa application requirements.
- You didn't show you had plans for your stay in France. No accommodation, flight tickets, or travel tickets had been booked. If the consulate doesn't believe you are coming to France for the reasons you have stated in your application they will reject the visa application.
- Your passport is either:

    A. invalid or expired
    B. will expire soon
    C. damaged
    D. Won't have 3 months remaining at the expiry date of the visa.
    E. Doesn't have two blank pages.
    F. You are considered to be a threat to France, or you have been involved in some fraud cases in the past. Visa applications from people with a criminal record will often be refused.

All rejections must be justifiable and you are entitled to a reason.

Here's what to do next

1. Read the refusal letter carefully – This will tell you the reason your visa was denied. It won't be specific but will give you a general reason for the refusal.
2. Can you fix the problem? – You may be able to provide more evidence to satisfy the French Consulate. You can reapply with the new evidence/documents.
3. Appeal – Some visa refusals can be appealed through an official process. It's important to read your rejection letter carefully and follow the appeal procedure exactly and within the stated time limits.
4. If your refusal letter indicates that it's not possible to appeal, you will have to reapply.

Should you appeal the rejection or apply again with new documents?

Your rejection letter will tell you if you are eligible to appeal the decision, and the procedures and deadlines for doing so.

There is no specific fee to appeal but you may have to pay for legal advice.

In many cases it will be easier to reapply with amended documents that remove the reason for rejection, rather than appeal.

The appeal process can take 2-3 months or even longer if your case is complex or the consulate is busy.

If you take it to court the process can take 6 - 12 months.

Appealing a visa refusal will be a different process depending on whether the visa is a short-stay or long-stay visa application.

Short Stay Visa Refusal Appeal

1.Submit an Informal Reconsideration Request (Free & Simple)

If you believe the refusal was a mistake (for example, if you did provide a required document but they overlooked it), you can write a polite email or letter to the French consulate that refused your visa asking them to reconsider. This is the French Consulate General in Washington (please note NOT the French Embassy).

This is an informal step, and while it's not guaranteed to work, some people have had success, especially for minor mistakes.

Your letter should contain the following information:

- Your personal details - name and surname, date and place of birth, passport number, and current address. Giving your email address and phone number is a really good idea too.
- At the beginning of your appeal letter, make sure you say when you applied for the visa, the date of

the visa rejection letter, any reference on the refusal letter and when you received it.
- Include the reason for your visa refusal. This is in the rejection letter you received.
- Explain why you think your application was wrongly rejected, and why they should approve it. It goes without saying that you should list all of the reasons why they should approve your application for a visa and the proof you have that shows their reasons for rejection are invalid.

2. Make an Official Appeal (If the Consulate Stands by Their Decision) - within 30 days of the original rejection letter being received

If your short-stay visa is formally refused and you want to challenge the decision, you can file an appeal with the Le Sous-Directeur des Visas (Deputy Director of Visas) in Nantes. You must do this before appealing to a court.

The address to send your appeal letter and documents to is: 11 rue de la Maison-Blanche 44036 Nantes Cedex 01 France

3. If the Appeal Is Rejected – Go to Court

If the Deputy Director of Visas rejects your appeal, you can take your case to the Tribunal Administratif de Nantes (Administrative Court of Nantes).

This is a legal process that may require a lawyer and could take months (6 - 12 months is an average timeframe).

It's usually only worth considering for serious cases where you have strong evidence that the refusal was unfair.

Long-Stay Visa Refusal Appeal

1. Submit an Informal Reconsideration Request (Free & Simple)

If you believe the refusal was a mistake (for example, if you did provide a required document but they overlooked it), you can write a polite email or letter to the French consulate that refused your visa asking them to reconsider. This is the French consulate in Washington DC (please note NOT the French Embassy)

This is an informal step, and while it's not guaranteed to work, some people have had success, especially for minor mistakes.

Your letter should contain the following information:

- Your personal details - name and surname, date and place of birth, passport number, and current address. Giving your email address and phone number is a really good idea too.
- At the beginning of your appeal letter, make sure you say when you applied for the visa, the date of the visa rejection letter, any reference on the letter and when you received it.
- Include the reason for your visa refusal. This is in the rejection letter you received.
- Explain why you think your application was wrongly rejected, and why they should approve it.

It goes without saying that you should list all of the reasons why they should approve your application for a visa and the proof you have that shows their reasons for rejection are invalid.

2. Make an Official Appeal (If the Consulate Stands by Their Decision) - within 30 days of the original rejection letter being received

If your long-stay visa is formally refused and you want to challenge the decision, you can file an appeal with the Commission de Recours contre les Décisions de Refus de Visa (CRRV) in Nantes. You must do this before appealing to a court.

The address to send your appeal letter and documents to is: CRRV – BP 83609 – 44036 NANTES CEDEX 1

3. If the Appeal Is Rejected – Go to Court

If the CRRV rejects your appeal, you can take your case to the Tribunal Administratif de Nantes (Administrative Court of Nantes).
This is a legal process that may require a lawyer and could take months (6 - 12 months is an average timeframe). It's usually only worth considering for serious cases where you have strong evidence that the refusal was unfair.

Just remember lots of people face delays or rejections and still end up in France. The key is not to panic - stay organised, persistent, flexible and polite.

Next up: Arriving in France

Let's Go

I should have done it sooner. I love the whole environment here. I love how calm I am. I love the culture and that the arts are more accessible here.

Congratulations! You've jumped through the visa hoops, dealt with the paperwork, and now you're holding that all-important sticker in your passport.

But before you celebrate too much, there are a few important things to do before you set off and when you arrive in France.

1.Check Your Visa Details

Before you even set foot in France, double-check your visa for any mistakes. Look at:

- Your name (is it spelt correctly?)
- Passport number (again, is it correct?)
- The visa type and duration (does it match what you applied for?).
- The validity dates (make sure you arrive before it expires!)

If you spot an error, contact the consulate before you travel to get it corrected.

2. Travel to France – What to Expect at the Border

When you arrive, you'll go through passport control. The officer might ask:

- Why you're coming to France
- Where you'll be staying
- Whether you have enough money to support yourself.

Be honest and confident, and keep key documents (like your visa approval, proof of accommodation, and return ticket) handy just in case they ask.

You can be turned away at the border even if you have a visa - it doesn't happen often, but it can.

Be prepared to show your passport with visa, any documents to prove finances to support you during your trip and health insurance.

3. Validate Your Visa (If Required)

Which Visas Need Validation?

If you hold a Visa de Long Séjour Valant Titre de Séjour (VLS-TS) (Long-Stay Visa Equivalent to a Residence Permit), you must validate your visa online within 3 months of arriving in France. This applies to:

- Work visas (employees, self-employed, Talent Passport)
- Student visas
- Visitor visas
- Spouse visas (for partners of French citizens)

How to Validate Your VLS-TS Visa

- Go to the official website: https://administration-etrangers-en-france.interieur.gouv.fr
- Provide your visa details: Enter your visa number, date of arrival, and personal information.
- Pay the validation fee: This varies depending on your visa type (usually between €50 and €200). You can pay online using a bank card.

- Receive confirmation: Once validated, you'll receive an official confirmation that serves as proof of legal residency.

What Happens If You Don't Validate Your Visa?

Failing to validate your visa on time means:

- You may be considered to be in France illegally
- You could have trouble renewing your visa or applying for residency later.
- You may face difficulties accessing healthcare, employment, or social services.

4. Other Actions You Might Need to Take

If your visa does not need online validation, you may still have to complete some formalities depending on your situation:

Applying for a Carte de Séjour (Residence Permit)

Some long-stay visas require you to apply for a Carte de Séjour (residence permit) at your local Préfecture. This applies to:

- Family reunification visas
- Certain work visas
- Retirement visas (this is a visa for foreign nationals who are entitled to a French state pension)

Your visa will usually mention 'une obligation de demander un titre de séjour' and you must apply to the prefecture for a residence permit within 2 months of arrival.

To apply, you'll usually need:

- Your passport and visa
- Proof of address in France
- Proof of financial means
- Medical certificate (if required by OFII)

5. Medical Visit and OFII Stamp

In some cases, you may be asked to attend a medical check-up organized by the OFII (Office Français de l'Immigration et de l'Intégration). This is common for work and student visas. You'll receive an appointment letter if required.

6. Open a French Bank Account

Many things in France (like renting an apartment or getting reimbursed for your medical expenses) require a French bank account. Some banks will let you open an account before you arrive, while others require proof of an address in France.

7. Apply for French Healthcare (If required)
If you're staying long-term, you need to register for French health insurance (Sécurité Sociale) through PUMA (Protection Universelle Maladie).

If you're working, your employer should help with this.

If you are registering as self-employed or starting a business this will trigger the application to PUMA automatically.

Everyone else needs to have been resident for 90 days in France before they can start their application.

In all cases, you must maintain your private health insurance until you are in the French system - it may take several months depending on your situation.

For more information about applying to be accepted into the French healthcare system please see the chapter entitled '*The French Healthcare System*'.

8. Settle Into Life in France!

Once the admin is sorted, it's time to enjoy your new life! Learn a few key French phrases, explore your local area, and embrace the quirks of French life - yes, even the long lunch breaks and endless paperwork!

Bienvenue! Welcome to France!

The French Healthcare System for New Residents

> We've been here 2 months now and I'm still in culture shock and wondering if I can adapt. Truly adapt.

One of the most important administrative tasks you will have to sort out when you arrive in France, is applying to be accepted into the French healthcare system.

France has one of the best healthcare systems in the world, offering high-quality medical care to residents.

However, if you're moving to France on a visa, you won't automatically be covered, and you'll need to apply.

This chapter will walk you through how the system works, what you need to do as a newcomer, and how to make sure you have access to medical care before you are accepted into the system.

Understanding the French Healthcare System

The French healthcare system, called Protection Universelle Maladie (PUMA), provides access to state-funded healthcare for residents.

Here's how healthcare costs are generally covered:

- The state usually covers 70% of medical expenses.
- For serious illnesses like cancer, diabetes, or heart disease, the state covers 100%.
- The remaining amount can be paid by you, or covered by a mutuelle (private top-up insurance).

Who Can Apply for French Healthcare?

As a third-country national (which includes US citizens), you won't automatically be covered for healthcare when you arrive in France.

You must go through an application process and be eligible.

To be eligible:

- You must work or reside in France on a stable and regular basis and have been resident in France for 3 months.
- You must have a residence permit (carte de sejour)
- You must live in France at least 6 months of the year (This may have tax implications).

Some people can apply immediately (without waiting for 3 months) including:

- Self-employed people and business owners – If you register as self-employed or set up a business in France, the process to join the French healthcare system is an automatic part of your business registration.
- Salaried employee

For everyone else, private health insurance is required until you're accepted into the French healthcare system, which can take several months.

You must maintain your private health insurance (if you visa required you to do this) until you receive your attestation des droits which is your proof of acceptance into the French healthcare system.

Step-by-Step Guide to Applying for Healthcare in France

Step 1: Make Sure You Have the Right Visa

To qualify for PUMA, you must be living legally in France with a valid long-stay visa (VLS-TS) or a residence permit (Carte de Séjour). When you apply, you'll need proof that you are a legal resident.

Step 2: Gather Your Documents

To apply for state healthcare, you'll need to submit a file to the Caisse Primaire d'Assurance Maladie (CPAM), which is the local health insurance office in your area. You'll need:

- A completed Demande d'Affiliation (application form for PUMA)
- A copy of your passport and visa/residence permit
- Proof of at least three months residence in France (unless you qualify for immediate access)
- Proof of income (such as payslips, tax returns, or pension statements)
- An RIB (relevé d'identité bancaire - French bank account details) for reimbursements. It must be a bank account in your name.
- A birth certificate (with an official translation if not in French)

Step 3: Submit Your Application to CPAM

Once you have all your documents, submit your application to your local CPAM office. Processing can take several months, so it's important to keep your private health insurance active until you receive confirmation.

You are waiting for an attestation des droits. This confirms your acceptance into the French healthcare system.

Step 4: Receive Your Social Security Number

Once your application is approved, you'll receive a temporary French social security number. This allows you to access the French healthcare system and get reimbursements for medical expenses.

At this stage, if you undergo any medical treatment, visit a doctor or get any medication from the pharmacy and pay for it, ask for a feuille de soins (brown form). You may have to pay upfront but this form will allow you to claim the state-covered costs back.

At some point you will be sent your permanent social security number and a letter to apply for your carte vitale.

Step 5: Your Carte Vitale

Your Carte Vitale is a green health insurance card that makes paying for healthcare easier. With this card, the state automatically covers its portion of medical costs, so you only need to pay your share.

To get your Carte Vitale, you'll need to:

- Wait for your permanent social security number to be issued (see above)
- Submit a photo and signature when requested
- Receive your Carte Vitale in the mail

Healthcare While Waiting for Approval

Since it can take several months to be accepted into the French healthcare system, you must have private health insurance during this waiting period unless you have one of the visas that didn't require private health insurance at the point of application.

Even if your visa application did not require private health insurance you are still expected to be able to cover all your medical expenses until you receive your attestation des droits, so you may want to consider taking out private health insurance for this period of time.

If you are one of the following, your right to French healthcare starts immediately BUT, as it takes several months to process this, you may be required to pay for any treatment or medications yourself up front. You should get a receipt (feuille de soins) and you can claim this back once you have received your attestation des droits.

- Self-employed people and business owners
- Salaried employee.

Once you are accepted into the French healthcare system, you can switch to a mutuelle (top-up insurance) to cover the costs that the state does not reimburse.

A mutuelle insurance is optional and you don't have to take one out.

The company you used for your private health insurance to get your visa will sometimes allow you to cancel the private health insurance and transfer to a mutuelle - so worth asking them.

Be aware however, that private health insurance that allows you to cancel early and swap to a mutuelle can sometimes be more expensive than a private health insurance policy that doesn't allow this.

How to Find a Doctor and Use the French Healthcare System

At the time of writing (January 2025) there is a shortage of general practitioners in many parts of France and especially in rural areas. You may find that many doctors aren't accepting new patients.

It is possible to see any doctor and there is a great service https://www.doctolib.fr/ that allows you to look for a doctor near you and make an appointment. Not all doctors are registered on this service though.

- Finding a Doctor: You can choose your own médecin traitant (general practitioner) and register them as your main doctor (if they are willing) to ensure better reimbursement rates. If you go and see a doctor that you haven't registered as your médecin traitant, the reimbursement rate will be lower.
- Seeing a Specialist: You usually need a referral from your GP to see a specialist but this is not always the case.
- Pharmacies: Prescription medications are partly covered by the state, and you will pay a reduced amount depending on the type of medication.

- Hospital Care: If you need hospital treatment, the state typically covers 80%, with the rest either paid by you or your mutuelle (if you have one).

Key Takeaways

- France's healthcare system is one of the best in the world, but you won't be covered immediately when you move.
- Most people must wait three months before applying, unless they qualify for immediate access (e.g. self-employed people).
- While waiting, you must maintain your private health insurance, (if it was a visa requirement), or the means to pay all your medical expenses until you are accepted into the French healthcare system. Even if you were not required to have private health insurance for your visa application you may want to consider taking this out to cover you until you are in the French system.
- Applications are made through CPAM, and the process can take several months.
- Once accepted, you'll receive a social security number and later a Carte Vitale for easier access to healthcare.
- The French state covers most medical costs, but you may want to get a mutuelle for extra coverage.

Mutuelle (Top-Up Insurance) – What You Need to Know

Let's talk about mutuelle, also known as top-up insurance. This is different from the private health insurance you needed to get your visa.

You can only apply for a mutuelle once you've been officially accepted into the French healthcare system and received your permanent social security number.

Unlike private health insurance, the cost of a mutuelle isn't based on your medical history—it's based on your age. This means the price will go up each year.

If you work in France, your employer must offer a mutuelle as part of your job. The company usually covers part of the cost, so it's worth asking your employer about the details.

There are different levels of coverage available, so you'll need to decide what works best for you. It's often a balance between cost and what's covered, so take your time to choose a plan that suits your needs.

Registering a Business in France

I just want to be honest about the whole process - it's so full of highs and lows - but overall it's a net positive to be sure!! You won't regret it!!

If you're planning to move to France to start your own business or work for yourself, this chapter will give you a handy overview of what you need to know.

While this book mainly focuses on visas, we'll cover the basics of setting up a business and the different business structures available.

Think of this as your starting point. Once you arrive in France with your Entrepreneur/Profession Libérale visa in hand, you'll have a clear idea of what to do next!

Choosing the Right Business Structure

France offers several business structures. It's worth looking at them all and deciding which one is best for you. Things to consider will be tax liability, social charges and whether or not you will need to hire an accountant (comptable) to prepare annual accounts.

It is possible, and sometimes compulsory, to change from one to another.

Here are the main options:

1. Micro-Entrepreneur (formerly Auto-Entrepreneur)

This is the simplest and most popular option for small businesses, freelancers, and self-employed individuals. It's ideal if you want a straightforward way to start a business with less paperwork. This is a popular option for people moving from the US.

Whilst it is the simplest one to set up, it may not be the best option for you overall.

Key Features

- Simplified tax and social security contributions
- No need for an accountant
- Easy online registration
- Turnover Limits: €77,700 for services eg. consultancy work, marketing services, gardening services etc) and €188,700 for trade (commercial retail). These figures are correct as of January 2025.

Once these limits have been met, you must change to one of the other available regimes.

It is important to realise that your tax liability and social contributions (cotisations) are based on your total turnover and not your profit.

Under the micro entrepreneur status you are not allowed to deduct expenses when calculating your tax liability and social security contributions. A flat rate is applied when you submit your annual tax declaration.

There are also thresholds for when you need to register for TVA (VAT).

At the moment (January 2025), this is €37,500 for services, €85,000 for businesses involved in any sales activity.
The French Government has very recently voted to reduce this threshold to €25,000 but on the 6th February this legislation was suspended pending further review.

Therefore at the moment the previous TVA thresholds remain.

Best for: Freelancers, consultants, small traders, and service providers.

2. Entreprise Individuelle (EI) - Sole Proprietorship

Similar to the micro-entrepreneur, but without revenue limits.

The main difference between this and a micro entrepreneur is that your tax liabilities and your social security contributions are based on profit rather than turnover.

Best for: Small businesses that may exceed micro-entrepreneur revenue limits.

3. EURL (Entreprise Unipersonnelle à Responsabilité Limitée)

A single-person limited liability company, where you are the sole shareholder.

Setting up and running an EURL is more complicated than for an ME or EI business.

An EURL requires the drawing up of company statutes, putting an announcement about its creation in the Journal D'annonces Légales and accounting requirements are more complex.

Best for: Individuals who want more legal protection and may hire employees.

4. SARL (Société à Responsabilité Limitée) - Limited Liability Company

A more structured business with two or more partners. It protects personal assets and follows corporate tax rules.

Corporation Tax is based on profits.

You are required to have a bank account in the business name.

Its operation is governed by law.

Best for: Small to medium-sized businesses with partners.

5. SAS (Société par Actions Simplifiée) - Simplified Joint-Stock Company

A flexible business structure with fewer formalities than a SARL. Can have one or more shareholders.
Best for: Entrepreneurs planning for growth or external investors.

SAS and SARL appear very similar at first glance. They both need a minimum of 2 partners. However, there are differences:

- SARLs are limited to 100 partners whereas a SAS has no limit
- SARLs operations are governed by law whereas a SAS has more flexibility in the way that it operates
- The role of the manager is different.

Steps to Register Your Business in France

Once you've chosen the right structure, you'll need to follow these steps:

1. **Choose a Business Name -** Make sure your desired name is unique by checking with the INPI (Institut National de la Propriété Industrielle) https://www.inpi.fr/

2. **Register Your Business Activity -** The Inpi website (see above) is a 'one-stop shop' for creating, modifying and ceasing your business activities. It is also the place to submit your annual accounts and other documents. Depending on the type of business, Inpi will pass your documents to the body responsible for your type of business who will issue you with a SIRET number, which is your official business ID in France.

3. **Register for Social Security and Taxes -** All business owners must contribute to the French social security system. Depending on your business type, you may be required to register for VAT (TVA).

4. **Open a Business Bank Account -** If you set up an EURL, SARL, SAS, or other company, you'll need a dedicated business bank account.

5. **Taxes and Social Contributions -** French businesses pay various taxes, depending on their structure.

Micro-entrepreneurs benefit from simplified tax payments based on revenue. Other business types may be subject to corporate tax (Impôt sur les Sociétés) or income tax (Impôt sur le Revenu).

Conclusion

Getting a visa that allows you to work or set up a business isn't the last step.

You must also follow the correct procedures for registering the business activity in France, although the new 'one-stop' shop has made that much easier than it was in the past.

Having made sure you have done everything you are supposed to do after your arrival in France, it's time to think of the language assessment and the medical if they apply to you.

Some of you will be exempt so you can skip the next Chapter - lucky you!

Language Test and Integration Into French Society

> My suggestion would be to move here if you want to live the life of a French person. If you want to reproduce your US or UK life in the in the French countryside, you'll likely be disappointed.

The French Government feels that greater integration into French society for foreign nationals is essential and have therefore introduced measures to make that happen.

These measures are mostly administered by **OFII**.

The Office Français de l'Immigration et de l'Intégration (OFII) is the French government agency responsible for immigration and integration services.

They are responsible for making sure that anyone moving to France meets the legal and administrative requirements for residency, work permits, and integration into French society.

They are the people that look after:

- The validation of your visa (if required)
- The French language test
- The medical examination
- The signing of the CIR (contrat d'intégration républicaine)
- The family reunification process
- The 4 day Civic Training Course (La formation civique)

The above administrative requirements are not required (other than the validation of your visa if required) for people with permission to reside in France for the following reasons:

- Visitor
- Student
- Intern
- Temporary Worker
- Fixed-term contract or secondment
- Seasonal worker
- Private and Family Life

If you are moving to France to take up permanent residency, you will almost certainly have some contact with OFII.

Language Requirements

The language levels mentioned here refer to the CEFR - an international standard for describing language ability. A1 is a complete beginner, C2 is native-level fluent.

There are 2 language levels you need to be aware of:

- The language level you have when called for your OFII interview after your arrival in France (if applicable). If it is not at A1 level you will have to agree to take French lessons.

- And secondly, your language level when you apply for any of the following:

  - A cartes de séjour pluriannuelles (multi-year residence permit). Currently you are required to have level A2 French when applying for this carte de sejour
  - A 10-year carte de résident (resident's card). Currently this is level A2.
  - French citizenship - the language requirement is currently B1

These levels are correct at the time of writing (January 2025).

However, from the 1st January 2026, new language requirements are being introduced.

- Multi-Year Residence Permit (Carte de Séjour Pluriannuelle): Language Requirement Increases from A2 to B1.
- 10-Year Resident Card (Carte de Résident): Language Requirement Increases from A2 to B1.
- French Citizenship: Language Requirement Increases from B1 to B2.

There are people who may be exempt from the language requirements:

- Applicants aged 65 or older (aged 60 for applications for French citizenship) Individuals with certified medical conditions that prevent language learning (a medical certificate is required)
- Holders of certain French diplomas or degrees or who hold a Diploma issued in French-speaking countries
- Residents under the Withdrawal Agreement Residence Permit (WARP) except for an application for French citizenship. (UK citizens only).

If you are working in France, either salaried or self-employed, you will have a training fund (this is one of the things that is paid for from your social charges/cotisations). You can use the money in this fund to finance French lessons from a recognized provider.

Conclusion

The interview at OFII is one of the things that people find the most frightening.

From the French side, OFII's role is to make your move to France as positive as possible, with an emphasis on integration into French life and culture which they see as including speaking French.

Renewing Your Visa/Carte de Séjour

> Sadly the inheritance tax laws are sending me back to the UK. I didn't do my research so can only blame one person!

Well, hasn't time flown?

You've been living your dream in France. Perhaps you've been renovating your dream property, or starting a business, or just travelling around France until you can decide where to put down roots.

No matter what you've been doing for the last 8 months, the time has come to think about renewing your visa or your carte de séjour residence permit.

Most types of visas are renewed online

https://administration-etrangers-en-france.interieur.gouv

However, some visas, including the VLS-TS entrepreneur/profession libérale, are renewed at your department prefecture.

You should start the renewal process no more than 4 months from the expiry date and no less than 2 months before the expiry date.

It's worth noting that it's common for your visa or carte de sejour to expire before you receive your renewal.

Required Documents

Each type of long-term visa renewal has slightly different requirements, but generally, you'll need the following:

- A completed application form (this varies depending on the visa type)

- A valid passport (original and copies)
- Recent passport-sized photos (meeting French ID photo standards)
- Proof of residence in France (utility bill, rental contract, or attestation from a landlord)
- Proof of financial means (bank statements, pay slips, pension proof, or financial support letter)
- Proof of health insurance. This will be private health insurance if not covered by the French system yet, or your attestation des droits which can be downloaded from the AMELI website in your personal space.
- Any additional documents specific to your visa type (for example, proof of student enrolment, work contract, or business activities)

Always check with your local Préfecture or the official government website for the most up-to-date list, as requirements can change.

The Process

Please note different prefectures have different ways of doing things (of course they do - it's France)! Do check on your prefecture's website for how to submit a request for renewal.

At your appointment, someone will review your documents and if everything is in order, you will be given a récépissé—a temporary permit allowing you to stay in France legally while your application is processed.

Processing times vary but can take anywhere from a few weeks to several months.

If your renewal has to be done on the ANEF website then you won't be given a récépissé. Instead ANEF issue different certificates depending on what is happening with your application:

- Certificate of Submission (when you submit your renewal application)
- Certificate of Extension (When your current carte de sejour has expired but they haven't processed your renewal yet (This grants permission to continue to reside in France whilst your application is being processed)
- Certificate of a Decision in Favour (This is for if the renewal has been granted but you haven't received your card yet).

What If Your Visa Expires Before The Renewal is Approved?

If your visa expires before your renewal is approved, don't panic! This is very common in France.

As long as you have applied before the expiration date and have received a récépissé or a certificate of submission you are legally allowed to remain in France.

As a US citizen and a beneficiary of the Schengen Visa Waiver, you can leave France whilst your renewal is being processed. However, you must be within the 90 days out of 180 days limit if you have been in another Schengen country.

You may find that border control stamps your passport when you return but this isn't a problem.

Common Pitfalls and How to Avoid Them

1. **Missing Deadlines**: Start early and keep track of your renewal timeline.
2. **Incomplete Documentation**: Double-check requirements and provide originals plus copies.
3. **Not Making an Appointment in Time**: Some préfectures have long wait times for appointments, so book early.
4. **Ignoring Changes in Rules**: French immigration laws can change, so always refer to the official government website (or check out the back cover of this guide for ways to get up to date information from me).
5. **Financial Stability**: If your income has decreased significantly, be prepared to show additional support documents.

What Happens If Your Renewal Is Denied?

If your renewal is denied, you'll usually receive a *refus de séjour* letter explaining the reason. You can appeal the decision within two months by filing a request with the Commission de Recours Administratif.

In some cases, seeking legal help from an immigration lawyer may be necessary.

Final Thoughts

Renewing your long-term French visa may seem like a daunting process, but with proper preparation, it can be relatively smooth.

The key is patience—after all, this is France, and bureaucracy is just part of the adventure!

Whilst I have taken great care to ensure that the information in this book is correct, immigration law is always evolving.

Scan Here

Subscribe easily

Keep up to date with any changes in the law or procedures by subscribing to our exclusive 'Moving To France' club.

Only €1.99 per month or €20 per year.

https://worldseyebooks.com/b/JUnT4

We will update you by email about any changes in the law or procedures that might affect you, and you will have access to our monthly webinars with experts on all things France.

You get the emails, the webinars with experts and you can message me with any questions and you can CANCEL ANYTIME.

Just scan the QR code or go to the website and pay securely via STRIPE, a highly secure payment platform trusted by businesses worldwide.

Key Terminology
For Visas

151When navigating the French visa system, you may come across various terms and definitions used by the authorities you will have contact with.

Understanding these key terms will help you make informed decisions and ensure that you choose the correct visa type for your situation.

The following section explains essential terms related to visas and residence permits.

Don't panic though! The various visas and residence permits will be covered in more detail as you go through this guide.

Visa - a document that gives permission to the holder to enter France and stay for a fixed period of time and under the terms and conditions related to that specific visa.

Visa de Court Séjour (Short-Stay Visa) – A visa that allows stays of up to 90 days within a 180-day period. This visa is commonly used for tourism, business trips, or family visits. US passport holders do not require this visa as the US is one of the countries that is exempt.

Visa de Court Séjour Travail - a visa that allows you to come and do temporary work lasting less than 90 days. This type of visa is usually issued for temporary assignments, short-term contracts, or specific events (like artists or sports professionals coming for an event).

Visa de Long Séjour (Long-Stay Visa - VLS) – A visa required for stays longer than 90 days.

Visa de Long Séjour Valant Titre de Séjour (VLS-TS) – A long-stay visa that also acts as a temporary residence permit, valid for up to one year. Holders must validate it upon arrival in France with the OFII (Office Français de l'Immigration et de l'Intégration).

Talent Passport (Passeport Talent) – A special visa category for highly skilled professionals, entrepreneurs, and investors moving to France for economic or research purposes.

Profession Libérale Visa – A visa for self-employed individuals or freelancers looking to work in France.

Titre de Séjour - a residence permit giving the holder the right to reside in France Anyone holding a Titre de Séjour has the right to reside in France. A validated VLS-TS is a Titre de Séjour, as is a Carte de Séjour and a Carte de Résident.

Carte de Séjour: Travailleur Temporaire (CDD) – A temporary worker residence permit issued to individuals employed in France under a fixed-term contract (Contrat à Durée Déterminée - CDD). This permit is valid for the duration of the contract, up to a maximum of 12 months, and is renewable if the employment continues.

Carte de Séjour: Salarié (CDI) – A residence permit granted to individuals with a permanent employment contract (Contrat à Durée Indéterminée - CDI). This permit is typically issued for one year initially and can be renewed for longer periods, leading to eligibility for a long-term residence permit.

OFII (Office Français de l'Immigration et de l'Intégration) – The French immigration office responsible for validating long-stay visas, medical checks, and integration procedures.

TLS - This is the visa application centre that handles your paperwork for your visa application. The French Consulate General in Washington DC however, processes and makes decisions on visa applications.

Temporary Residence - residents whose residence permit must be renewed. For example, the VLS-TS/Carte de Séjour-Visiteur usually needs renewing each year for the first 5 years of residency.

Permanent/ Long-term Residence - After 5 qualifying years in France, residents can apply for a Carte de Résident. This gives permission for the holder to reside in France permanently.

Regroupement Familial (Family Reunification) – A process that allows foreign residents in France to bring their family members to live with them under specific conditions.

Schengen Zone – A group of European countries that allow free movement across their borders for short stays.

TCN (Third Country National) - This term is used for anyone who is coming to France and is not from an EU/EEA member state. This includes the US.

Autorisation de Travail - work permit. This is applied for by a prospective employer in France. The application must be made and be successful before you can apply for your visa.

CDI (Contrat à Durée Indeterminée) - a permanent employment contract

CDD (Contrat à Durée Determinée) - a fixed or temporary work contract

SMIC (Salaire Minimum de Croissance) - minimum wage in France. The SMIC rates change every year so it's important to use the current rate when working out what the minimum financial requirements are for your visa application. (The gross amount is before any deductions are made, the net amount is after social contributions, pension, and unemployment contributions have been deducted).

Jeune Entreprise Innovante - Young Innovative Company. This is defined as: "A new company that invests in research and development (R&D) has the status of a young innovative company (JEI), a young university company (JEU) or a young growth company (JEC)". This is referred to in the section on Talent Passports.

Profession libéral - There are 2 types of professions libérals - regulated and unregulated.

Regulated professions libérals include (but not restricted to):

- Doctors, dentists, midwives, pharmacists, and veterinarians

- Lawyers, auctioneers, bailiffs, notaries, court clerks, and judicial administrators.
- Architects, land surveyors, and chartered accountants are among the key experts in this domain.

Unregulated professions libérals include (but not restricted to):

- all professions which are not commercial, craft, industrial or agricultural and which do not form part of the regulated liberal professions.

PACS (Pacte Civil de Solidarité) - The French equivalent of a civil partnership that provides legal recognition of the partnership plus some financial and tax benefits.

CESEDA (Code de L'entrée et du Séjour des Étrangers et du Droit d'Asile) - French Immigration Code

RÉCÉPISSÉ - A receipt that is given when you apply to renew your residency permit.

CIR (Contrat d'intégration républicaine) - This is a contract you are asked to sign that is between you and France

Whilst I have taken great care to ensure that the information in this book is correct, immigration law is always evolving.

Scan Here

Subscribe easily

Keep up to date with any changes in the law or procedures by subscribing to our exclusive 'Moving To France' club.

Only €1.99 per month or €20 per year.

https://worldseyebooks.com/b/JUnT4

We will update you by email about any changes in the law or procedures that might affect you, and you will have access to our monthly webinars with experts on all things France.

You get the emails, the webinars with experts and you can message me with any questions and you can CANCEL ANYTIME.

Just scan the QR code or go to the website and pay securely via STRIPE, a highly secure payment platform trusted by businesses worldwide

A Word From the Author

If you have found this guide helpful I'd be grateful if you would write me a review that I can use in my publicity.

You can do this in any (or all) of the following ways:

✽ Please leave a review on Amazon.com, amazon.co.uk or amazon.fr

✽ For those of you who are members of various Social Media Groups for people planning to, or thinking about, moving to France, please recommend my book (if the rules of the particular group allow you to do this).

✽ If you would like to give me any feedback please email me isabellabirdauthor@gmail.com

Many thanks and I wish you well as you embark on your new adventure. Bon Courage!

www.ingramcontent.com/pod-product-compliance
Lightning Source LLC
LaVergne TN
LVHW052048070526
838201LV00086B/5062